Classics in Psychology 1855–1914

A Collection of Key Works

Thoemmes / Maruzen

Classics in Psychology, 1855–1914

A Collection of Key Works

Edited by **Robert H. Wozniak,** *Bryn Mawr College*

Robert H. Wozniak, *Guide to Classics in Psychology, 1855–1914* (1999)

1. A. Bain, *The Senses and the Intellect* (1855)
2. H. Spencer, *The Principles of Psychology* (1855)
3. A. Bain, *The Emotions and the Will* (1859)

4/5. G. T. Fechner, *Elemente der Psychophysik* (1860)

6. F. Galton, *Hereditary Genius* (1869)
7. H. Maudsley, *Body and Mind* (1870)
8. H. Taine, *On Intelligence* [1870] (1871)
9. H. L. F. Helmholtz, *On the Sensations of Tone* [3rd ed., 1870] (1875)
10. W. Wundt, *Grundzüge der physiologischen Psychologie* (1874)
11. W. B. Carpenter, *Principles of Mental Physiology* (1874)
12. F. Galton, *English Men of Science* (1874)
13. D. Ferrier, *The Functions of the Brain* (1876)
14. G. H. Lewes, *The Physical Basis of Mind* (1877)
15. T. Ribot, *German Psychology of To-Day* [1879] (1886)
16. R. H. Lotze, *Outlines of Psychology* [1881] (1886)
17. J. H. Jackson, *Evolution and Dissolution of the Nervous System* [orig. pts, 1881–7] (1932)
18. H. Höffding, *Outlines of Psychology* [1882] (1891)
19. F. Galton, *Inquiries into Human Faculty and Its Development* (1883)
20. H. Ebbinghaus, *Memory* [1885] (1913)
21. H. Bernheim, *Suggestive Therapeutics* [1886] (1889)
22. A. Binet, *The Psychology of Reasoning* [1886] (1899)
23. E. Mach, *Contributions to the Analysis of the Sensations* [1886] (1897)
24. G. T. Ladd, *Elements of Physiological Psychology* (1887)
25. G. J. Romanes, *Mental Evolution in Man* (1888)
26. C. L. Tuckey, *Psycho-Therapeutics* (1889)

27/28. W. James, *The Principles of Psychology* (1890)

29. W. Wundt, *Lectures on Human and Animal Psychology* [2nd ed., 1892] (1894)
30. P. Janet, *The Mental State of Hystericals* [1892–4] (1901)
31. O. Külpe, *Outlines of Psychology* [1893] (1895)
32. J. M. Baldwin, *Mental Development in the Child and the Race* (1895)
33. C. L. Morgan, *Habit and Instinct* (1896)
34. E. B. Titchener, *An Outline of Psychology* (1896)
35. W. Wundt, *Outlines of Psychology* [1896] (1897)
36. J. M. Baldwin, *Social and Ethical Interpretations in Mental Development* (1897)
37. L. T. Hobhouse, *Mind in Evolution* (1901)
38. E. L. Thorndike, *An Introduction to the Theory of Mental and Social Measurements* (1904)
39. M. Prince, *The Dissociation of a Personality* (1906)
40. O. Pfungst, *Clever Hans (The Horse of Mr. Von Osten)* [1907] (1911)
41. A. Forel, *The Senses of Insects* (1908)
42. E. B. Huey, *The Psychology and Pedagogy of Reading* (1908)
43. W. McDougall, *An Introduction to Social Psychology* (1908)
44. W. D. Scott, *The Psychology of Advertising* (1908)
45. M. F. Washburn, *The Animal Mind* (1908)
46. R. Schulze, *Experimental Psychology and Pedagogy* [1909] (1912)
47. E. Claparède, *Experimental Pedagogy and the Psychology of the Child* [1910] (1911)
48. E. L. Thorndike, *Animal Intelligence* (1911)
49. H. Münsterberg, *Psychology and Industrial Efficiency* (1913)
50. E. L. Thorndike, *Educational Psychology* (1914)

Dates in square brackets indicate the original French or German editions from which these first English translations were prepared.

Psycho-Therapeutics;

Or, Treatment by Sleep and Suggestion

CHARLES LLOYD TUCKEY

THOEMMES PRESS

MARUZEN CO., LTD

This edition co-published in 1998 by

THOEMMES PRESS
11 Great George Street
Bristol BS1 5RR, United Kingdom

&

MARUZEN CO., LTD
3–10, Nihombashi, 2-chome, Chuo-ku
Tokyo, 103–8245 Japan

Psycho-Therapeutics
ISBN 1 85506 678 5

Reprinted with kind permission of the
Trustees of the National Library of Scotland

Classics in Psychology, 1855–1914
50 volumes : ISBN 1 85506 602 5

British Library Cataloguing-in-Publication Data
A CIP record of this title is available from the British Library

Printed in England by Antony Rowe Ltd, Chippenham

Publisher's Note

The Publisher has gone to great lengths to ensure the quality of this reprint but points out that some imperfections in the original book may be apparent.

This book is printed on acid-free paper, sewn, and cased in a durable buckram cloth.

PSYCHO-THERAPEUTICS;

OR,

TREATMENT BY SLEEP AND SUGGESTION.

BY

C. LLOYD TUCKEY, M.D.

LONDON:
BAILLIÈRE, TINDALL, AND COX,
20 & 21, KING WILLIAM STREET, STRAND.
1889.

TO

DR. LIÉBAULT,

OF NANCY,

IN ADMIRATION OF HIS GENIUS,

THIS SMALL BOOK

IS

Gratefully Dedicated.

PREFACE.

In bringing forward this little book on Treatment by Suggestion, I feel that, though I must crave indulgence for the shortcomings of the writer, no apology is necessary for introducing so important a subject.

The Nancy treatment has during the last few years attracted so much interest among men of science and members of the medical profession on the Continent, that it seems strange the knowledge of it in this country is almost entirely theoretical. The system of psycho-therapeutics has so far attained its fullest development in Holland, where in every large town it is followed by at least one well-qualified practitioner; while in Germany, Russia, Sweden, and indeed every European country, its position is secured by the support of leading physicians, and by the success attending their practice. In every country, I believe, the introduction of the system was at first opposed by persons who feared the popularization of so potent an agent; but as the beneficial results of the treatment became manifest opposition decreased, and has now almost died out. This is doubtless due chiefly to the fact that the treatment has not been allowed to fall into the hands of ignorant and unqualified practitioners, but has been accepted by men of high character and professional repute. The dangers of hypnotism have been proved chimerical; in proper hands no undesirable medical results can occur through its practice, and there is, I believe, hardly one authenticated case of its being used for a criminal purpose in the countries where it is most frequently employed by medical men. More than this can hardly be said for any system of medical treatment.

But while maintaining that hypnotism has been very little used for criminal purposes, we should be foolish to blink the fact that it *might* conceivably, under certain circumstances, be a dangerous weapon in unprincipled hands, and that its injudicious use *might* lead to physical and mental ills; but such evil results are in a very great measure preventible. Wherever hypnotism has been largely adopted as a valuable aid in the treatment of disease, its importance has been formally recognised, and its employment by charlatans, either as a toy at public exhibitions, or in unauthorized medical practice, has been prohibited by law.

Medical electricity is only now emerging from the limbo of quackery, because for years the medical profession allowed it to be exploited by 'professors,' who used it as a universal remedy in all cases, suitable and unsuitable. The Nancy system has been successful on the Continent because it is practised there by qualified physicians and surgeons, whose knowledge and experience has taught them where the treatment would be likely to succeed, and where it would prove ineffectual. I here advocate its use not as a universal remedy or as a supplanter of ordinary medical treatment, but as a powerful auxiliary in combating many forms of disease not readily reached by other means.

My best thanks are due to Dr. Donald Baynes for his kindness in correcting proofs.

CHARLES LLOYD TUCKEY.

14, GREEN STREET,
GROSVENOR SQUARE,
Jan. 1st, 1889.

CONTENTS.

CHAPTER IV.

CHAPTER V.

INTRODUCTION.

It is now nearly thirty years since Dr. Liébault began to treat patients in a public dispensary at Nancy by a new system, which he gradually elaborated, and caused to be known as *Treatment by Suggestion.*

In 1866 he published a book on the subject, in which he gave to the world a full description of the means used by him, and an account of cases successfully treated.* But little notice was taken of it at the time, and even in Nancy, where Dr. Liébault lived a retired life, devoted to the poor among whom he practised, he was regarded as, at the best, an amiable but mistaken enthusiast. In 1882, Professor Bernheim, of the Faculty of Medicine at Nancy, began to investigate the system, quite as a sceptic, so he tells us, and, being soon convinced of its value, introduced it into his hospital *clinique*. In 1884 he brought out his classical work on suggestion.†

Dr. Bernheim was well known in the medical world, and his book attracted general attention on the Continent.

* 'Du Sommeil et des Etats Analogues, considérés surtout au point de vue de l'action du Morale sur le Physique,' Paris, 1866.

† 'De la Suggestion, et de ses Applications à la Thérapeutique,' Paris (second edition), 1887.

His example was soon followed by other physicians and writers of eminence, among them Professors Beaunis* and Liégeois,† of Nancy, Delbœuf,‡ of Liège, Burot and Bourru, of Rochefort, Fontain and Sigard, of Bordeaux,§ Forel, of Zurich; and Drs. Despine, of Marseilles, Van Renterghem and Van Eeden, of Amsterdam, Wetterstrand, of Stockholm, Schrenck-Notzing, of Leipsic, etc. The literature of the subject published in French alone during the last five years would make a fair-sized library; and almost every large town on the Continent has its practitioners of the system, who nearly all have written about it more or less extensively. Also, a journal‖ is published monthly in Paris, in which its latest developments are fully described and discussed.

So far as I know, there is in English no literature on the subject treated therapeutically. From time to time articles have appeared in the medical and scientific journals, especially in *Brain* and *Mind*, alluding to its progress abroad, and giving reviews of some of the foreign books relating to it. The Psychical Society have investigated the phenomena of suggestion from a purely scientific standpoint, and Dr. Hack-Tuke led up to its very threshold in his deeply interesting work.¶

* 'Du Somnambulisme provoqué,' Paris, 1886.

† 'De la Suggestion et du Somnambulisme dans leur Rapports avec la Jurisprudence et la Médecine légale,' Paris, 1888.

‡ 'De l'Origine des Effets curatifs de l'Hypnotisme,' Paris, 1887.

§ 'Eléments de Médecine Suggestive.' Paris, 1887.

‖ *Revue de l'Hypnotisme*, Paris, 170, Rue S. Antoine.

¶ 'Illustrations of the Influence of the Mind upon the Body' (second edition), London, 1884.

To James Braid, the Manchester surgeon, is due the credit of having seen the germs of truth which lay hidden and obscured in the writings of Mesmer and the animal magnetizers. He attempted to explain by physical laws the effects produced by mesmerisers,* and he ridiculed the notion of there being any such thing as a magnetic fluid or current. His disgust for the mysticism of mesmerism drove him, perhaps, too far towards the other extreme, and made him more rationalistic than the facts warranted him in being. Although he publicly demonstrated his system of healing—which he practised with much success—and wrote several works upon the subject, it appears to have died with him, and it remained for Dr. Liébault to arrive at the truth of psycho-therapeutics.

I believe that all great discoveries are led up to by previous half-discoveries; and it does not detract from Dr. Liébault's credit that he started with a large amount of evidence on the subject collected by earlier observers, any more than Darwin's claim to be the first evolutionist is weakened by his having drawn on the material supplied by Lyell, Hooker, and a multitude of others. Liébault's genius taught him to arrange and systematize the facts collected by his predecessors, and to find the true explanation of phenomena which they had misunderstood. And his patience and steadfast courage led him to persevere in his work, undeterred by opposition or neglect, until now

* 'Neurypnology,' London, 1843; 'The Power of the Mind over the Body,' London, 1846.

we find him the founder of a school which, as I have said, has its representatives all over the Continent—acute and clear-sighted men of science, of a class quite unlikely to entertain the fanciful theories of mesmerism, on the one hand, or those of 'faith healing,' on the other.

TREATMENT BY SUGGESTION.

CHAPTER I.

ALL who have given any attention to the subject acknowledge what immense power the mind—acting in conjunction with or apart from the will—has over the body, forcing it at times to unusual or even extraordinary effort. This power is exercised both in health and disease, but is peculiarly evident—perhaps because it is more closely observed—in the latter condition. Everyone, physician and psychologist especially, knows some curious instances illustrative of its effects: such as the story of the hospital patient to whom the consulting physician gave a prescription, with the remark, 'Take this, it will do you good.' At the man's next visit, he, being asked for the prescription, replied that he had swallowed it as directed, and it had, according to promise, done him 'a power of good.' Dr. Hack Tuke (*op. cit.*) gives a number of cases in which drugs have acted not according to their proved properties, but according to the expectation of the patient. For instance, a student having asked for an aperient pill, the dispenser by mistake gave him one composed of opium and antimony, which, instead of producing the usual effect of inducing perspiration and drowsiness, acted in the way the student expected. Every medical man can quote examples of this sort from his own practice, and if sometimes he is wrongfully accused of having produced baneful effects, he is indemnified at others by having marvellously good results ascribed to very simple measures.

There are few cases of this kind more remarkable than one related by Mr. Woodhouse Braine, the well-known chloroformist. Having to administer ether to an hysterical girl who was about to be operated on for the removal of two sebaceous tumours from the scalp, he found that the ether bottle was empty, and that the inhaling-bag was free from even the odour of any anæsthetic. While a fresh supply was being obtained, he thought to familiarise the patient with the process by putting the inhaling-bag over her mouth and nose, and telling her to breathe quietly and deeply. After a few inspirations she cried, 'Oh, I feel it; I am going off!' and a moment after her eyes turned up, and she became unconscious. As she was found to be perfectly insensible, and the ether had not yet come, Mr. Braine proposed that the surgeon should proceed with the operation. One tumour was removed without in the least disturbing her, and then, in order to test her condition, a bystander said that she was coming to. Upon this she began to show signs of waking, so the bag was once more applied, with the remark, 'She'll soon be off again,' when she immediately lost sensation, and the operation was successfully and painlessly completed. This girl had taken ether three years before, so that expectation and the use of the apparatus were sufficient to excite her recollection, and call back the effects of the drug as then experienced.

It is told that when Sir Humphrey Davy was investigating the properties of laughing-gas—as nitrous oxide was then called—he proposed to administer it to a man who was suffering from tic doloreux, but before doing so he tried his temperature by putting a thermometer into his mouth. The man took this instrument for some new and subtle remedy, and in a few minutes exclaimed that the pain was cured. The same belief in the efficacy of the thermometer remains to this day among the uneducated, as a friend of mine found to his cost when he was hospital-clerk to a well-known physician. It was his duty to take each morning the temperature of every patient; but on one occasion, being pressed for time, and knowing by experience that a certain patient's temperature was always normal, he saved a few minutes by leaving it untried. Later in the day, when the physician asked this man how he felt, he replied that he was much worse, as might be expected considering the way in which he was neglected. On inquiry it came out that the potent charm of having the glass tube in his mouth for three minutes had been omitted, and my friend got a reprimand.

While in Jamaica, I knew a young lady who had for months been confined to her bed or couch, unable to walk a step, from apparent paralysis of the lower extremities, which entirely defied the treatment used. One morning news was brought to her that her brother, to whom she was devotedly attached, had fallen from his horse, and was lying in a critical condition some miles away in the mountains. She immediately got up, herself helped to saddle a horse, rode to the scene of the accident, and nursed her brother night and day for a week. She was completely and permanently cured of the paralysis, which of course was merely functional and hysterical, by the nervous shock which had brought her will into operation.

A somewhat similar case came under my observation some years ago. A clergyman in whose house I was staying had long been a sufferer from chronic rheumatism, through which he was so disabled that he could only walk very slowly and with great inconvenience. On this occasion he was lying on a sofa, from which he could see through an open door and across a hall into another room, where his wife happened to be. By some careless movement she upset a table there, and, as if by magic, he sprang to his feet and walked rapidly and with a perfectly even step into the opposite room, exclaiming, 'There goes all the ink that was in the house, and I have to write my sermon!' In this instance, however, the cure was as ephemeral as the emotion which had caused it; but it is not improbable that a continued excitement might have prolonged the power of easy motion, and so have broken down and caused absorption of the adhesions and exudations which produce the pain.

At a water-picnic some months ago, a young lady complained of terrible neuralgia. From some cause the boat began to rock violently, and she became extremely nervous. Her fear of being upset completely drove away the neuralgia, which did not return, at least on that occasion. It is known that sufferers from sea-sickness almost invariably become quite well in moments of danger; and we can often lose the sense of pain by occupying our mind with some affair of great interest.

On the other hand, it is possible for an apparently quite healthy person to develop, by pure imagination, the symptoms of serious illness. Laymen who dabble in medical science, and medical students at the beginning of their course, are apt to imagine that they have one or other of the diseases they have been studying—heart-complaint being perhaps the most usual; and of this they do frequently develop some of the subjective symptoms.

A friend of mine tells me that once only in his life has he suffered from laryngitis and loss of voice. This was while attending Dr. Semon's lectures on diseases of the throat. It may have been a mere coincidence, but that hardly explains the frequent instances of medical men who have succumbed to the disease which they have made their special study, *e.g.*, Professor Trousseau from cancer of the stomach. It is probable that the mind being continuously fixed on one special organ, predisposes to disease of that organ.

Hypochondriasis is, as we know, a condition in which the patient feels the working of his internal organs, and is morbidly conscious of them. It tends to grow worse, because his attention becomes more and more fixed upon functions which ought to be performed automatically, and unless some powerful mental stimulant is applied, organic disease is sometimes actually set up. There are many people, of both sexes, who never hear of a disease without fancying they have it. The illness of a royal or distinguished sufferer, the progress of which is daily recorded in the newspapers, will sometimes become almost epidemic; thus throat specialists can tell some curious stories of the increase of imaginary and real throat-affections during the illness of the late Emperor Frederick; and a short time ago, it will be remembered, measles became for a while a fashionable malady. That fear will promote disease has been abundantly proved during outbreaks of cholera, small-pox, the plague, and other epidemics. Pseudo-hydrophobia is a recognised malady, and no doubt many supposed cures of hydrophobia have in fact been cures of this fear-induced imitation.

We sometimes come across people who tell us they 'have no time to be ill;' and certainly reports of longevity show that rust destroys more than use, and that hale old age is more frequently attained by those who have led busy lives than by idlers. Idleness is a well-known factor in producing all kinds of ailments, real and imaginary, of mind and body, perhaps because the idle man, from sheer lack of interest in life, devotes too much attention to his own organism.

Imagination, combined with 'direction of consciousness' (Sir H. Holland) to a past, will produce results which have been noticed by many pathologists. John Hunter said he was confident of producing a sensation in any part of his body simply by concentrating his attention on it. Sir H. Holland observes*: 'In hypochondriasis, the patient, by fixing his attention on internal organs, creates not merely disordered sensations, but disordered action in them.' And again: 'When there is liability to irregular pulsation (of the heart), this is brought on and increased by a simple effort of attention.'

A medical friend of mine, who is affected with insuffi-

* 'Medical Notes and Reflections,' London, 1839.

ciency of the mitral valves, tells me that he is hardly ever inconvenienced by it, except when he has to examine a patient with heart-disease. His attention is then drawn to his own weakened organ, and he suffers from palpitation.

Dr. Forbes Winslow, speaking on this subject, says*: 'It is a well-established fact that alterations of tissue have been the result of a morbid concentration of the attention to particular organic structures. Certain feelings of uneasiness or even pain originate in the mind a suspicion of disease existing in particular parts of the body, it may be in the lungs, stomach, heart, brain, liver, or kidneys. Some slight irregularities and functional disturbances in the action of these organs being noticed, are at once suggestive (to the hypochondriac) of serious and fatal disease being established in the part to which the attention is directed. This deviation from a normal state of certain functions frequently lapses into actual *structural* disease, as the effect of the faculty of attention being for a lengthened period concentrated on this action. The continuous direction of the mind to vital tissues *imagined* to be in an unhealthy state undoubtedly causes an exaltation of their special functions, and an increase of susceptibility, by (it may be presumed) concentrating to them an abnormal quantity of blood, this being followed successively by (1) undue vascular action, (2) capillary congestion, (3) an excess in the evolution of nerve force, and (4) appreciable *structural* alterations.' Dr. Hack Tuke says†: 'If twenty persons fix their attention on their little finger for ten minutes, the result will be that most of them will feel decided sensations there, amounting in some to a mere sense of weight or throbbing, and in others to actual pain.' He endeavours to explain this by supposing that the act of attention excites an increased flow of blood to the part, and consequent increased vascularity of the sensory nerve-ganglia, so leading to subjective

* 'Obscure Diseases of the Brain and Mind,' London, 1860.

† *Op. cit.*

sensation; or that the sympathetic nerve-centres become excited, and the vaso-motor nerves influenced thereby so as to cause in the finger temporary vascular changes which invoke sensation. He puts forward also a third hypothesis, which is interesting from the relation it bears to that given by Professor Delbœuf, of Liège (see page 71)—that fixing the attention on a part of the body for some time renders us conscious of the working of functions which are usually performed automatically and unconsciously. Sir James Paget thinks that by nervous excitement the temperature may be raised to at least 101 (from the normal 98½); and Professor Wunderlich says on the same subject*: 'In hysterical neurosis elevations of the temperature even to excessive heights may occur without any motive at all.' Dr. Wilkes relates cases of extreme anæmia caused by depressing emotions; and this agrees with the experience of all medical men, as does also the opposite observation, that pleasant emotions bring about a good state of the blood and secretions, and improve the health. Instances in which the hair has rapidly, even in a few hours, suffered atrophic changes, leading to its becoming white and falling out from excessive depressing emotions, are common; and under similar circumstances the teeth will sometimes rapidly decay.

Dr. de Watteville says†: 'One of the most striking properties of the nervous system is that by which the activity of one portion may be arrested or prevented—"inhibited"—by the activity of another . . . when we attend closely to a sensory impression or to a train of thought, the excitability of every part of the brain, except that actually engaged in the act, is diminished by an inhibitory action of the working portion. Thus when we say that anger or fear paralyses, we allude in very accurate language to the inhibitory influence which powerful emotion exercises on the cerebral functions.' That emo-

* 'Medical Thermometry,' New Sydenham Society, 1871.
† 'Sleep and its Counterfeits,' *Fortnightly Review*, May, 1887.

tion and fancy have power to modify the secretions is shown by the well-known fact that the mouth becomes dry and parched through fear or anger, while on the other hand it 'waters' at the idea of savoury food; the mental impression paralysing or stimulating the secretory apparatus of the salivary glands. Violent emotion, again, will so modify the secretion of gastric juice as to cause indigestion in subjects at all predisposed to it. An attack of jaundice may be induced by anger—as the popular saying, 'Green with rage,' implies—from an accumulation of bile in the blood through nervous excitement causing 'inhibition' of the secretory function of the liver.

Disease, then, as we have seen, may, in hypochondria and kindred states, be induced by *auto-suggestion*, and there is no doubt that it may likewise be induced by suggestion from without. Let a man be told repeatedly by his friends that he is looking ill, that he does not seem fit to go about, that he must take care of himself, or he will have this or that complaint—and unless he has a very cheerful and well-balanced mind, he is pretty sure, for a time at least, to deteriorate in health. There is a story of such suggestions being made, for a practical joke, at the expense of a stalwart farmer, who, having been assured by several persons that he seemed in a bad way, did really take to his bed and go through an unmistakable attack of illness. This of course was a cruel and unwarrantable jest—yet a somewhat similar effect is occasionally produced by well-meaning persons, who are in the habit of commiserating their acquaintance for not looking well.

Dr. Hack Tuke gives an instance of death itself being produced by suggestion. A Frenchman of rank was condemned to death for some crime, and his friends, willing to avoid the scandal of a public execution, allowed him to be made the subject of an experiment. He was told that he must be bled to death. His eyes were bandaged, and his arm having been lightly pricked, a stream of warm water was made to trickle down it and fall into a basin, while the assistants kept up a running commentary on his supposed condition. 'He is getting faint; the heart's action is becoming feebler; his pulse is almost gone,' and other remarks of the sort. In a short time the miserable man died with the actual symptoms of cardiac syncope from hemorrhage, without having lost a drop of blood. (*Vide* note in Appendix, page 69.)

There are some authenticated cases of apparent death being produced by auto-suggestion. We hear of this being accomplished by Indian fakirs and other religious enthusiasts in Eastern countries. Braid cites a remarkable, and, he believes, thoroughly well-authenticated instance of a distinguished holy man, who, to convince an incredulous Indian prince that he possessed this power over himself, apparently died, and was laid in a sealed coffin within a vault, the entrance to which was also sealed and guarded by soldiers. After six weeks, the time appointed by himself, he was taken out of the tomb in the presence of the Rajah and of several credible witnesses, English as well as native, and found to display every appearance of death. Having been gradually revived by his own servant, the still ghastly-looking, corpse-like creature sat up and spoke, his first words being addressed to the doubting Rajah: 'Do you believe me now?'

The best warranted European case of the sort is that of Colonel Townshend, related as follows by Dr. Cheyne: 'He could die or expire when he pleased, and yet, by an effort or somehow, he could come to life again. . . . We all three felt his pulse first; it was distinct, though small and thready, and his heart had its usual beating. He composed himself upon his back, and lay in a still posture for some time. While I held his right hand, Dr. Baynard laid his hand upon his heart, and Mr. Skrine held a clean looking-glass to his mouth. I found his pulse sink gradually, till at last I could not feel any, by the most exact and nice touch; Dr. Baynard could not feel the least motion in the heart, nor Mr. S. discern the least soil of breath on the bright mirror. Then each of us by turns examined his arm, heart, and breath, but could not, by the nicest scrutiny, discover the least symptom of life in him. We reasoned a long time about this odd appearance, and, finding he still continued in that condition, we began to conclude that he had indeed carried the experiment too far; and at last we were satisfied that he was already dead, and were just ready to leave him. This continued about half an hour. . . . As we were going away we perceived some motion about the body, and, upon examination, found his pulse and the motion of his heart gradually returning; he began to breathe heavily and speak softly. We were all astonished to the last degree at this unexpected change.'*

As sickness, and perhaps even death, may be produced by suggestion, so may be, and very often is, produced the cure of sickness. Towards this, however, auto-suggestion, though it might do much, does actually little or nothing, the natural reason being that the mind of a sick person, when left to itself, is prone rather to suggest morbid than health-inducing ideas, and so operates for mischief rather than in the direction of cure. Every physician knows how, by determined hopefulness and cheerfulness, a sufferer from functional, and even from curable organic disease, may facilitate the work of healing, and materially hasten his recovery.

In all ages wonderful cures, real amid a multitude of shams, have been wrought at holy places dedicated to various saints of various cults. Among the throngs of pilgrims to Mecca, to the sacred rivers and temples of India, to the shrines of Buddhist hagiology, there are some who, having made the outward journey wearily and painfully, do indeed turn homeward with the gift of health. A proportion of those who have limped or been carried to Lourdes and to a hundred other holy places of the Catholic Church, do leave behind them crutches that they no longer

* In the article on 'La mort simulée' ('Dict. Encyclop. des Sciences Médicales,' Paris, 1875), Dr. G. Tourdes refers to some similar cases, and endeavours to explain them scientifically.

require. Some of the sufferers who worshipped the Holy Coat at Trèves, did truly receive in restored health the reward of their faith. Some wearers of relics and amulets are really the better for possessing them. The cheered, uplifted, and convinced mind works, sometimes with startling rapidity, on the diseased body.

For this same reason, touching for the king's evil did no doubt effect many cures. The royal progresses were announced some time before hand, and the sufferers along their route had often weeks in which to cherish the expectation of healing, in itself so beneficial; and in those days of faith, when a belief in the divine right of kings was universal and strong, the touch of the royal hand must, except in the most hopeless cases, have had a stimulating effect which may often have caused a healthful reaction. Even in our own times, a royal touch, accompanied by kindly words, has good effect. We read in the life of Victor Emanuel,* that in 1865, when the cholera was raging in Naples, and the panic-stricken inhabitants were migrating by thousands from the city, the king, wishing to give his people courage, went the round of the hospitals. 'He stood beside the sick-beds, and spoke encouragingly to the patients.' Before one of those already marked for death, the king stopped, and taking his damp, frozen hand, he pressed it, saying, 'Take courage, poor man, and try to recover soon.' The warm grasp of the hand, the strong cheerful words, the recognition of the king's face, had an agitating effect on the dying man. That evening the syndic visited the king, and said: 'Your majesty's coming is a joyful omen. I am happy to tell you that the doctors report a diminution of the disease in the course of the day, and your majesty has unawares worked a miracle. The man you saw this morning stretched for death is out of danger this evening. The doctors say the excitement of your presence caused the salutary crisis.' In Carpenter's Physiology† numerous

* 'Life of Victor Emanuel,' by G. S. Godkin, vol. ii., p. 213.

† 'On the Influence of the Nervous System on the Organic Functions,' chap. v., ninth edition.

examples are given demonstrating the influence of the mind and imaginative faculties on the different bodily functions, and we have only to consider a moment to recall many personal experiences pointing in the same direction.*

* My friend, Dr. Roth, the well-known pioneer of Ling's Swedish gymnastics in England, to whom I owe my introduction to Dr. Liébeault and his system, tells me he has been using suggestion without hypnotism all his life, and we know that a main object of Ling's method is to evoke the patient's dormant will-power.

CHAPTER II.

I HAVE endeavoured to show how much the imagination (in its widest sense) may have to do with our health of mind and body; and I shall now try to point out that the effects of 'directed consciousness' are greatly increased under certain conditions, when the mind is so withdrawn from the consideration of all extraneous ideas as to be absolutely concentrated upon one object.

We have seen how concentration of mind-faculty, whether self-induced or brought about by some shock to the system, or some powerful external influence, can modify functions, and both produce and cure disease —sometimes gradually, but often, in the case of shock or sudden and overpowering influence, with a rapidity which seems almost miraculous.

We all know, and frequently by our own experience, that mind-concentration, brought about by some strong motive, will enable us to perform mental or bodily actions of which we would generally be incapable. Through it a man will achieve feats of strength far beyond his apparent muscular power, or will go boldly through dangers from which he would shrink if he paused to consider probable consequences. Or he will, in a limited time, execute a prodigious amount of intellectual work, possibly of such startling excellence that he himself, in after-moments of less intensity, will be amazed at his own performance. Of course concentration, if sustained at such a pitch, would in time be the ruin of mind and body; but we know that it is a necessary factor in the accomplishment of all great things, and that there can be no success in life for those who cannot command it to a moderate degree. Of this, we see a striking instance in Coleridge, who, with all his wonderful genius, brought a surprisingly small quantity of work to completion, for want of this mind-directing power. The less we have of it, the more our mental action tends to become automatic. The mind of a person unused to exercise it, drifts undirected and undisciplined from one idea to another; he can hardly follow a line of thought to its conclusion, and his talk, and probably his actions, will be as inconsequent as his wandering fancies.

As a rule, happily, the organic functions which carry on life are purely automatic; but, as we have seen, it is possible to concentrate the attention upon them, and so affect their operation, sometimes beneficially, but far more commonly with detriment to the health of mind and body. Those bodily movements over which we have full control are also generally performed automatically. Under ordinary circumstances, we give no conscious thought to our steps in walking, to the motion of our hands while at work; these are nearly as automatic as healthy breathing. So likewise, in a general way, is the operation of the senses. We see, hear, feel without any effort of our will, unless some special motive impels us to exercise it. We concentrate our minds upon sight when we strive to see a minute, or indistinct, or distant object; and upon hearing when we listen for a faint or eagerly-expected sound. If such concentration is continuously brought to bear upon any sense, it will in time convey automatically the more intense impression which has been exceptional. Thus, in savages and in travellers and settlers in wild or dangerous regions, the senses of sight and hearing are far more keen than in those who live under civilization. The senses of touch and hearing become exquisitely fine in the blind. A blind man will sometimes hear sounds which are absolutely inaudible to ordinary ears, and recognise objects by touch as correctly as most people can by eyesight. Some blind persons seem, through concentration, to have developed a sense of space. On entering a room they can tell whether few or many persons are present; they can guess with wonderful accuracy the size and shape of an enclosed place, and have a curious power of avoiding any obstruction, such as an article of furniture which may be in their way.* Deaf people often develop the sense of sight to an extraordinary extent. By concentration of this faculty they are able, as we know, to follow a speaker by watching his expression and the motion of his lips. Their sense of touch also becomes more delicate; and occasionally they are able to enjoy music by feeling the vibration of air set in motion by its sound.

Concentration of mind upon intellectual or physical action is usually possible only in our waking and wakeful moments. Fatigue of brain renders us incapable of it; and in sleep, the natural consequence of such fatigue, we generally lose consciousness, and only exercise those functions which are performed automatically. In dreams consciousness is once more aroused, and we may even use some reasoning power, and be influenced from without through our senses. But in ordinary dreams there is no concentration of ideas upon an act to be performed or a goal to be reached. When a sleeper uses this effort of mind, he passes out of the region of dreams, and enters that of somnambulism.

The somnambulist never has that semi-consciousness of his state, and of the unreality of his fancies, which sometimes exists through a dream—when the sleeper *knows* that he is dreaming, and will even try to prolong his vision if it be delightful, and dispel it if painful. Such an exertion of will is impossible in somnambulism.† In this state all fancies *must* appear realities. The imagina-

* Most people have probably noticed that closing the eyes will, for the moment, render the hearing and touch unusually acute. Any sense may be intensified by mind-concentration, as in the case of tea and wine tasters, and of professional buyers of raw silk, who develop an unerring capacity of judging its quality by touch.

† In dreams, doubtless, it is possible only when the sleeper is close upon waking.

tion is, as I have said, concentrated upon one object, and so completely that actions are as effectually performed as if directed by strong will-power. But an onlooker can easily perceive, by the expression and posture of somnambulists, that the discerning and judging faculties are in abeyance.

In somnambulism actions of extraordinary difficulty, such as could not be performed by the sleeper during his waking hours—except, perhaps, through mind-concentration caused by some overpowering impulse or motive—are accomplished with perfect ease. Persons in this condition will walk on the extreme edge of a precipice, climb dangerous heights, get out of a house through an upper-story window. There are numerous instances of this on record, of which I will quote two or three. Dr. Paul Garnier* gives one of a patient, a dentist's assistant, of feeble bodily and mental health, who frequently fell into a state of somnambulism. On one of these occasions he escaped by a window from the ward of the Hôtel Dieu, in which he was undergoing treatment, and, though a peculiarly unathletic person, walked easily and fearlessly along the sloping parapet of the façade—a feat which a trained gymnast could hardly have accomplished. He awoke in the course of this dangerous performance, and had to be rescued by means of a ladder. With the return of consciousness reason awoke, and he understood the horror of his position. While blindly obeying his impulse he had acted automatically, and fear, which is a product of reflection and association of ideas,† had no existence for him.

A patient of my own, a young man twenty years of age, not an habitual somnambulist, but a sufferer from nightmare produced by chronic dyspepsia, on one occasion, while spending the night in an hotel, dreamed that he was

* 'Somnambulisme devant les Tribuneaux,' Paris, 1888.

† Infants, in whom of course neither is possible, will, if allowed, grasp at the flame of a candle, or a sharp instrument; and young children will fearlessly put themselves into positions of great danger.

confined in a dungeon from which he must escape. The dream no doubt passed into somnambulism, for under its influence he broke his iron bedstead—a feat of strength which, waking, he assuredly could not have accomplished—and tore up his bed-clothes. His amazement was great when he awoke in the morning amid the ruins of his own creation. He remembered his dream, but had no recollection whatever of the acts into which he had been led by it.

Dreams thus merging into somnambulism may produce tragic results. Dr. G. Tourdes* relates how a man sleeping beside his wife dreamed that she was a robber whom he must kill. He accordingly attempted to suffocate her with a pillow, and it was with great difficulty that she succeeded in awaking him, and so saving her life.

In 1843 a young man was tried for the attempted murder of an innkeeper at Lyons.† He had arrived at the inn towards nightfall, and was allotted a room. In the dead of night loud cries were heard from this room, and the landlord, rushing in to see what was the matter, was set upon by his guest and seriously wounded. It was ascertained that the young man was a somnambulist, who had dreamt that the landlord was murdering the occupants of a room near his own, and that he was defending them. He was, of course, acquitted.

We have many instances of mental work being accomplished during somnambulism. Professor Wœhner‡ of Gottingen, after vainly trying for several days to write a Greek poem on a given subject, composed it successfully while in this condition, which probably was brought about by the mental strain of his previous futile efforts.§

A clear case of somnambulism was that of a clergyman,

* Article 'Sommeil,' 'Dictionnaire Encyclopédique des Sciences Médicales.'

† 'Dictionnaire Encyclopédique des Sciences Médicales,' article 'Somnambulisme,' by Drs. Ball and Chambard.

‡ 'Dictionnaire Encyclopédique,' etc.

§ Coleridge's poetical fragment, 'Kubla Khan,' was probably composed in a dream—not in somnambulism—as he remembered and wrote it down on awaking.

whom his wife saw rise from bed in his sleep, go to a writing-table, and write rapidly for some minutes. This done, he returned to bed, and slept on until morning. On awaking, he told her that in a dream he had worked out an argument for a sermon, of which he now retained no recollection whatever. She led him to the writing-table, and showed him the written sheet, upon which he found his argument worked out in the most satisfactory manner.

It rarely happens, however, that solutions of problems, poems, etc., written by persons in this state, have any value. They may begin well, but generally drift into nonsense, probably because the mental concentration has been dispelled by some new idea crossing the first, and displacing it.

Habitual somnambulism may be natural—that is, may exist without any actual disease, though it is hardly ever found in persons of robust bodily and mental constitution. It is not uncommon in delicate or nervous children and young persons, but if with advancing years the mind and body gain strength, the tendency to it is likely to decrease and finally disappear. *Accidental* somnambulism is directly produced by illness or mental strain, and may occur in normally healthy persons of great intellectual power. When the state is habitual or frequent, the somnambulist may be said to lead two lives, one almost distinct from the other, and to have two entirely unconnected memories. Memory, as we generally understand it, is dormant during somnambulism. The sleeper remembers nothing that has occurred during his waking hours, and, when he again awakes, has no recollection of his actions during the somnambulistic state. Yet, in his next attack of somnambulism, the memory of these is likely to come back to him.

The effect of natural or accidental somnambulism on the health is anything but beneficial. An attack is generally followed by feelings of weariness and discomfort, for which the subject is at a loss to account. The concentrated mind-power does not operate in a beneficial direction, but impels the sleeper to bodily or mental effort likely to have an exhausting and hurtful effect upon him. But the artificially-produced mental condition seen in hypnotism can be turned to therapeutic uses, and be made to fill a void which no other plan of treatment can reach. Dr. Bernheim considers hypnotic sleep analogous to the natural state, with the important difference that in natural sleep the subject is only in relation with himself, whereas in the artificial state he is in relation with the operator, who is therefore able to direct the thoughts into the channel he wishes. That it resembles natural sleep is proved by the fact that it is possible in certain cases for one to pass into the other. Dr. Van Eeden told me that a patient of his, a gentleman, wearied by long waiting and exhausted by the heat, fell asleep in the waiting-room. The doctor came in, and, seeing him asleep, said, 'Don't wake, but come with me into my consulting-room.' The patient got up and, with assistance, did as he was desired. After the treatment was over he was led back in the same way to his former seat in the waiting-room, and allowed to finish his sleep. He soon awoke, apologized to the other patients for having slept, and expressed surprise that his turn had not yet come for seeing the doctor. Great was his astonishment when he was told that the séance had taken place and was finished without his knowing anything about it. Dr. Maury,* who cannot be accused of being too easily influenced, gives some instances in which, while sitting by his fireside dozing after dinner, he had heard, as in a dream, the words uttered by his wife and friends, and had followed out the train of thought suggested by them in his dreams, and had even acted upon suggestions so made.† If a person is very tired it is frequently possible to obtain

* 'Le Sommeil et les Rêves,' Paris, 1865, p. 429.

† He relates how, on one occasion, he was sitting in his easy-chair half awake, when his wife spoke to him. He was awakened by the words, and remembered them, but was quite unable to tell whether he had uttered them himself, or whether they were his wife's. On this he remarks, 'How many actions and ideas are daily suggested to us by others which we act upon, thinking they are our own!'

an answer to a question whispered in his ear without awakening him. Dr. Hack Tuke and Mr. Braid give several examples of this in their writings.

Braid, for instance, tells of a naval officer who was the subject of many practical jokes. He entertained and acted upon any idea which was suggested to him when asleep without awaking. On one occasion, while lying in his berth, he was told that his ship was in action, and that his men were fighting all around him. His face immediately assumed an expression of martial excitement, and he wielded an imaginary sword. His friends supplied details of the fight, telling him that the battle was going against them, and that his dearest companions were being killed; then his expression changed to one of fear. Finally, when told that all his friends were slain, and that the rout was complete, he leaped from his place and fled with an aspect of terror. I have myself spoken to and received answers from nurses who had fallen asleep, worn out by long hours of watching; and examples of such automatic answering must be familiar to most people. On the other hand, patients in the hypnotic sleep sometimes pass into the natural state, when they are no longer in relation with the operator, but follow their own ideas in ordinary dreams.

As in natural somnambulism a person may be able to do things he is at other times incapable of; so in the artificially-produced condition he can sometimes be made to excel himself. Dr. Beaunis found in experimenting with the dynamometer that the muscular power could be greatly increased at times by suggesting in the hypnotic state increased strength and effort; and one frequently finds the grasp of an enfeebled patient can be perceptibly strengthened by similar suggestions. The therapeutic bearing of this experiment is easily seen.

Dr. Grazzini, of Florence, has kindly sent me some copies of drawings done while in a state of hypnotic somnambulism by an uneducated man who in waking moments hardly knew the use of a pencil. These copies are faithfully and well executed, but probably the man would have been quite unable to initiate a design. The faculty of imitation was strengthened by the hypnotic condition, and at the same time he concentrated all his attention on the figures, and took infinite pains to reproduce them.

An artist under the same circumstances would no doubt have produced a drawing in his usual style; and a musician in a similar way, if asked to play, would perform some familiar air. Whatever a man's natural disposition might be it would come out if he were in a state of profound hypnotic sleep; but we shall see that 'suggestion' in this condition has power to modify even life-long habits and deep-rooted tendencies.*

* Frequent repetition of the suggestion, especially if done with confidence, has what may be called a cumulative action, expressed by Professor Delbœuf in a kind of mathematical formula. This, of course, is also the case in our waking moments, and is well understood and turned to account by advertising tradesmen. The announcement in confident language on every blank wall that 'Johnson's soap is the best,' becomes, by constant repetition, almost an axiom, and we are inclined to accept its truth. In the same way it is told of George IV. that from constantly repeating the story of his being at Waterloo, he at length got to believe that he had really taken part in the battle.

CHAPTER III.

I HOPE to have shown in the preceding chapters that Dr. Liébault's system is the outcome of the collection and classification of many isolated facts previously neglected or misunderstood. That cures have been and still are worked by such means as are implied in faith-healing, the mind-cure, etc., and by charms and relics, is beyond doubt; but it is not in the supernatural that we should seek for the explanation of them. They all proceed from the same cause, and on the same lines. We have, firstly, the patient's strong desire for cure; and, secondly, his firm belief in the efficacy of the means used; while to these may generally be added the presence of a sympathetic and impressive environment. The reasonable and deliberative side of the patient's brain is suppressed, while the emotional or instinctive side is developed, and in proportion as the latter is predominant the greater generally is the success of the treatment. The Nancy school obtain, in suitable cases, as good results as it is possible to expect; but they work on scientific principles and by recognised laws.

A brief account of the treatment practised at Nancy, and of the theory which explains it, will, I think, make this clear.

If the visitor to Dr. Liébault's dispensary be one who measures results by the impressiveness of the means used, he will surely be disappointed to find how commonplace are operator, patients, and building. The rooms are unpretentious, and even shabby; the patients are ordinary-looking people enough, belonging mostly to the artisan and labouring classes; and the doctor himself, though he has goodness and kindliness written on every feature, is of unimposing presence; while his habit of chatting on all sorts of subjects with the persons around him, even while receiving patients, has an odd and hardly impressive effect.

The patient paying his first visit is directed to sit down and watch the treatment being applied to others. This gives him confidence, and arouses that imitative faculty, which is so active in childhood and is never lost throughout adult life. When his turn comes, he is told to take his place in an arm-chair, and to make his mind as much a blank as possible—'to think of nothing at all'—and to fix his eyes and attention on some special object; almost anything will do, from the operator's face or hand to a mark on the ceiling or the pattern of the carpet. Then the phenomena which attend the on-coming of natural sleep are gradually 'suggested' to him: 'Your sight is growing dim and indistinct; your eyelids are becoming heavy; a numbness is creeping over your limbs; my voice seems muffled to you; you are getting more sleepy; you cannot keep your eyes open.' Here the eyes close of themselves, or are closed by the operator, and it is generally found that the patient is indeed asleep.

About two minutes of this 'talk about sleep' will usually produce the hypnotic effect on a new patient; and on subsequent visits even less time is required.

The patient being more or less influenced, Dr. Liébault now proceeds with the treatment proper. This consists essentially in directing the invalid's attention to the part affected, and suggesting an amelioration or disappearance of the morbid condition and symptoms. To take a very simple case—let us suppose that the malady is chronic nervous headache. The part of the head affected is gently rubbed, so that the patient's attention shall be attracted to it, and he is told that the pain is to disappear—that he will awake feeling his head cool, clear, and comfortable, and that there is to be no return of the trouble. In ordinary cases the whole process will not have lasted more than five minutes when Dr. Liébault brings it to a close by arousing the patient, which he does by telling him to open his eyes and awake. This is generally enough ; he awakes as from ordinary sleep, and is told to vacate the armchair in favour of the next patient. When asked how he feels, he will generally reply that he is better, and very often that the pain has entirely vanished. He is quite his natural self, and can leave the room at once and go about his work as usual. Long acquaintance with the system prevents an inhabitant of Nancy from regarding it as anything remarkable, and a sick person consults Dr. Liébault just as he would consult any other physician, with the simple idea that the treatment will do him good. He does not trouble himself with metaphysical theories, but is content to know that some acquaintance has been cured of a complaint similar to his own, and that he himself hopes to be relieved in a few days.

If the hypnotic sleep has been profound, it may be necessary twice or thrice to repeat the order to awake, and even to enforce it by fanning the patient, or blowing gently upon his eyes ; but the simple command is nearly always sufficient.

There certainly is nothing mysterious in all this, and Dr. Liébault seems to take pleasure in making his whole mode of treatment clear to any serious inquirer, and in giving the rational explanation of everything that he does. He directs the patient to fix his attention on a certain point in order to strain the accommodation of the eyes and tire the sight. The effect of the strain is to cause dilatation of the pupils and consequent dimness of vision. The feeling of heaviness in the eyelids results from the fatigue of keeping them open in a strained position, and the assertion that the eyes are becoming tired and the sight dim is therefore founded on physiological data, and is not guesswork. The eyes being tired, the natural impulse is to close them, and this act calls up a previous association of ideas connected with fatigued or confused sight. That association points to sleep, towards which the patient is rapidly led, aided by the monotonous tones of the operator suggesting it to him, and by his mind being free from all disturbing thoughts, and his nerves from all external stimuli. He falls asleep, in fact, much in the same manner as one does when reading a dull book or listening to a not too brilliant discourse. Dr. Maury,* in his well-known work on sleep and dreams, says, 'The less the mind is occupied with ideas the more easily can the thoughts be directed into any given channel. If nothing claims our notice or holds our attention, the cerebro-spinal system, for want of that gentle stimulation which is necessary to it, falls into a state of semi-torpor inseparable from atony of the nervous system.'

In the chapter on sleep in Carpenter's 'Physiology,' various conditions are mentioned as being favourable to it, one being the desire for it, another the expectation of it. We expect, from previous experience, that if we lie down in a certain place, sleep will follow. The faculty of imitation helps to bring it about; when we see others dozing we naturally incline to follow their example, and at night the consciousness that all around us are asleep disposes us to seek the same condition. Talking about sleep is apt to induce somnolence, just as talking about food may provoke hunger. And a monotonous sound, such as the droning voice of a speaker, or the breaking of gentle waves upon the seashore, tends to encourage slumber. Thus it will be seen how closely the artificial method I have described follows natural rules. This method may fail, just as we may fail to obtain natural sleep, or may battle it off should we desire to remain awake. If a patient wishes to resist the somnolent influence, he can do so by refusing to concentrate his thoughts, or by inducing some physical discomfort—for instance, by placing himself in an uncomfortable position. Strong emotion, such as anger or fear, will prevent the hypnotic sleep; so will severe pain, hunger, thirst, and indeed anything which preoccupies the mind or agitates

* 'Le Sommeil et les Rêves,' Paris, 1865.

the nervous system. Constitutional idiosyncrasies affect this as they affect the natural sleep. The naturally restless sleeper will be restless, and he who commonly goes off as soon as his head touches the pillow will quickly succumb to the hypnotic influence. The extent to which a person is influenced varies according to his mental and physical condition. If he is of restless and flighty temperament it may be impossible to fix his attention for even the few minutes that are necessary, and no effect is produced—except, perhaps, an inclination on his part to treat the whole affair as a jest, and a consequent irritation on the part of the doctor. But in ordinary cases some effect is certainly produced, if not on a first visit, still on subsequent ones. This effect will vary in various patients, some feeling only a heaviness and torpor, with a disinclination to open the eyes, while others fall into a more or less profound sleep, or into a state of somnambulism. Dr. Liébault divides the sleep into six different stages,* but as these really merge imperceptibly into each other, the division is purely arbitrary and is made for convenience in classification. They may be shortly summed up as: 1. Light sleep; 2. Profound sleep; 3. Somnambulism.

The first and second stages closely resemble and are analogous to ordinary sleep; but the third is *sui generis*, and will require a few words later on.† Though it is analogous to natural sleep, there is one very important fact which shows that the conditions are not identical. If an ordinary sleeper is spoken to, he is generally aroused by the stimulating effect of the sound conveyed to the brain through the auditory nerves, but one in the hypnotic state may be talked to without being disturbed—the effect will, on the contrary, be soothing. He is, in fact, *en rapport* with the outer world, though only to a limited extent, whereas in natural sleep he is *en rapport* only with his own consciousness.

Upon this difference depends the possibility of applying curative suggestion. Carpenter (*op. cit.*) says that the

* See Appendix, p. 75, note 6. † See Appendix, p. 71, note 5.

very closure of the eyes renders the other senses more acute; and we have seen that the inactivity of one sense is nearly always compensated for by increased sensitiveness of the others. Now in the hypnotic state all the senses are more or less torpid and in abeyance until called into play by the operator. Physiologists suppose that during activity the nerve-centres are continually discharging nervous energy in all directions in response to stimulating impressions received through the senses; but in sleep a state of inactivity is induced, and the nervous force accumulates in the brain-cells. Natural sleep comes as a consequence of fatigue, and because the store of nerve-energy is nearly or entirely exhausted. During its continuance a fresh store of nerve-energy will be laid up, and if it be undisturbed, this store will go on increasing until sufficient is acquired for complete nerve recuperation. This point attained, the sleeper, if in good mental and bodily health, will awake naturally, and feel no further desire for slumber. But as the hypnotic state may be produced at any time in the twenty-four hours, and long before any perceptible inroad has been made on the store of nerve-energy laid up during the previous natural sleep, it follows that during the artificial sleep there may be great accumulation and excess of energy. All this can be concentrated and directed into any channel the physician may desire; and this concentrated and directed nerve-force must naturally affect the system more powerfully than any ordinary nervous impression. This fact may explain the rapid production of congestion to a given part (alluded to in Chapter IV.), and also the sensation of warmth usually experienced in any part to which the attention has been drawn. It also accounts for the success of the treatment in paralysis of long standing.

We may imagine in such a case, and the surmise would probably be physiologically correct, that the nervous channels are blocked to ordinary impulses sent to them from the brain, but that the extraordinary impulse from an accumulation and concentration of nerve-force is sufficient to break down and overcome the obstruction; as a dam which easily withstands ordinary currents is swept away upon the bursting of a reservoir, by the rush of accumulated water.

Bernheim defines hypnotism as *the production of a psychical condition in which the faculty of receiving impressions by suggestion is greatly increased.* But this is only half the truth; for not only is the receptivity increased, but the power to act upon and carry out the suggestion is increased likewise. Suggestions have all the force of commands, and the patient will strain every nerve to obey them. If he is told to move a paralyzed limb, or to speak after months of loss of voice, one can see what intense effort he puts into the attempt to comply. A stammerer making such effort will speak fluently, and a deaf person will distinctly hear a whisper. To express adequately the cause of such effects, the word 'suggestion,' in English at least, is far too weak, and therefore somewhat misleading.

The increased force of suggestion does not depend so much as one might suppose on the profoundness of the sleep. In the case of deafness, referred to above, the hypnotic effect was extremely slight; and, on the other hand, I have heard a person in a state of decided somnambulism argue with the operator as to the correctness of his assertions. In applying suggestion, all that is necessary is a state of increased receptivity of ideas suggested by the operator, and an ignoring of other impressions. This attained, it matters little from a therapeutic point of view whether light sleep, profound sleep, or somnambulism, is produced. My own experience, like that of all observers whom I have known, is that good results are effected when there has been no loss of consciousness, and even when the patient denies having felt any hypnotic influence.*

* A gentleman, whom I am treating for various nervous affections, always denies having slept, and protests that he has remained con-

Consciousness is lost only in the advanced stages of profound sleep, and even when this has occurred there is remembrance on waking of everything that has happened during the sleep. A patient in profound sleep may be questioned, and will probably return answers, unless the question be put too brusquely, when it will be likely to wake him, or too gently, when he may shirk replying; for a person in this state dislikes being disturbed, and is especially unwilling to exert his reflective faculties. Nevertheless, if questioned as to his complaint, he will give truthful replies, and thus may help the physician in his diagnosis and treatment.

Bernheim seems to accept the theory of Herbert Spencer,* and of most psychologists, that two sorts of nervous action go on within the brain—the one automatic and instinctive; the other rational, volitional, and deliberative. Hypnotism suppresses the latter (the *Ego* of some psychologists), and allows full play to the former.† It follows that where the second kind of nervous action prevails in an individual, he is less liable to be acted upon by external impressions, and is less the creature of impulse than one in whom the first kind is predominant. The more a man's actions are the result of impulse rather than of reason, the more susceptible he is to external impressions, and therefore to suggestive treatment.‡

This brings us to the question, Who are the best subjects for the treatment, and how far is it applicable to the bulk of mankind?

Professor Charcot asserts that it is suitable, and indeed possible, only for hysterical subjects. He divides the

---

scious of everything going on around him. Yet if I put some small article, such as a paper-knife, into his hand during the sleep, and tell him to hold it tightly, he will do so, and on being aroused will show surprise at finding himself grasping it.

* 'Principles of Psychology.'

† See Appendix.

‡ He who obeys his instincts, and instantly knocks down a man who has insulted him (this being a purely automatic action), would thus be a better subject for hypnotism than he who deliberately calls a policeman and goes in for damages.

hypnotic sleep into three well-defined stages: 1. Lethargy; 2. Catalepsy; 3. Somnambulism; and contends that there is a regular sequence in these, and that, according to the will of the operator, one or other can be produced.*

Drs. Liébault, Bernheim, Beaunis, and others of the Nancy school deny the existence of these three stages. They assert that their experience in treating hypnotically a vast number of patients leads them to the conclusion that nothing resembling them has been or can be evoked *spontaneously*. They consider, in fact, that Professor Charcot has introduced a new hysterical condition into the Salpêtrière, and that this has become as it were an institution of the place which every new-comer hastens to comply with. They support this assertion by showing that when they in their Nancy practice explained to hysterical patients the effects produced by Charcot, the three stages, never before manifested, were forthcoming. Bernheim has well said: 'Méfiez-vous de la suggestion;' and an English physician has given an equally sage warning: 'Take care, or you will find what you are looking for.'† Charcot has thus entered the field weighted with a theory which he seems unable to shake off. If one of his school is shown a broad-shouldered navvy or a sun-dried

* He obtains a state of lethargy by fixing the patient's eyes on a given point, or by gentle pressure on the eyeballs. This state resembles natural profound sleep. It passes into the second stage when the eyelids are opened: cataleptic rigidity may now be produced in a limb, and it may be bent or placed in any position. Moreover, emotions corresponding with the position are evoked. If the subject is put into a pugilistic attitude, his expression will become fierce and determined; if into one of prayer, it will wear the aspect of devotion. The third stage is produced from the first or second by gently rubbing the top of the head, when the cataleptic condition will vanish, and other characteristics will appear, chief among which are abnormal acuteness of the senses, and obedience to suggestion. The reader must be struck by the artificial nature of these stages.

† Braid was at one time misled into supposing that by touching the phrenological 'bumps' he produced corresponding effects. For instance, if he touched the 'bump' of Destructiveness, the subject immediately proceeded to hit out and to destroy whatever was within his reach; if that of Benevolence, he would give away his watch, purse, etc., to any bystander. The fact is, that the sense of sight (under the apparently closed eyelids), that of hearing, etc., are so abnormally acute in somnambulists, that the slightest hint of expression, voice or touch, is sufficient to evoke from them the desired response.

old soldier in a state of profound hypnotic sleep, and is asked whether this looks like an hysterical subject, he will reply that appearances are deceptive, and that the very process of hypnotising has developed a latent condition of hysteria, or one analogous to it. To my mind the great merit of Dr. Liébault is, that he approaches the subject with only one end in view—the relief of disease. If the theories he has deduced from observed facts (for every man who is not a mere empiric must hold theories) do not, after closer observation, continue to correspond with them, the theories are thrown over, and not the facts, as too often happens. The Nancy school may therefore be called practical and therapeutic, in distinction from Charcot's, which is theoretical and experimental.

The following table, taken from Professor Beaunis' work, proves what a mistake it is to suppose that only hysterical persons are influenced by the treatment.

Patients submitted to hypnotisation by Dr. Liébault in 1880 (1,014):

Not influenced	27
Drowsiness	33
Light sleep	100
Heavy sleep	460
Very heavy sleep	232
Somnambulism (slight)	31
Ditto (advanced)	131
	1,014

Professor Beaunis shows as follows the percentage of the different stages of hypnotism at different ages:

	Somnambulism.	Very heavy sleep.	Heavy sleep.	Light sleep.	Drowsiness.	Uninfluenced.
To 7 years	26·5	4·3	13	52·1	4·3	—
7 to 14 "	55·3	7·6	23	13·8		—
14 " 21 "	25·2	5·7	44·8	5·7	8	10·3
21 " 28 "	13·2	5·1	36	18·3	17·3	9·1
28 " 35 "	22·6	5·9	34·5	17·8	13	5·9
35 " 42 "	10·5	11·7	35·2	28·2	5·8	8·2
42 " 49 "	21·6	4·7	29 2	22·6	9·4	12·2
49 " 56 "	7·3	14·7	35·2	27·9	10·2	4·4
56 " 63 "	7·3	8·6	37·6	18·8	13	14·4
63 and above	11·8	8·4	38·9	20·3	6·7	13·5

These statistics refer, of course, to Nancy, and, as has been already pointed out, that town is pervaded by an atmosphere of hypnotism and suggestion. But my friend Dr. Van Eeden assures me, that at Amsterdam he finds the proportion of the 'uninfluenced' but little larger. The proportion of somnambulists, however, is undoubtedly much greater at Nancy than we could expect to find it in England. Among about fifty patients I have as yet found only two or three.

And here a word on the subject of somnambulism. As natural somnambulism is nearly always associated with mental or bodily weakness, so the artificial variety is, I believe, found chiefly in patients whose minds are weakened by hysteria or an allied nervous condition, or whose bodies are enfeebled by phthisis or some other wasting disease. It is an abnormal product of hypnotism, and, interesting though the phenomena may be from a pathological and psychological point of view, they are no more a part of suggestive treatment than an exhibition of the poisonous effects of drugs is a part of ordinary medical practice. They help to elucidate points in the treatment, and therefore must be studied, but experimentation upon them is outside the scope of the physician, as such.*

* See Appendix. Hypnotism being a new thing in England, the knowledge of it seems chiefly confined to theory, and one has to hear many fanciful and exaggerated statements. For instance, in an article on the subject in the *Saturday Review* of December 8th, 1888, *à propos* of a paper of mine in the *Nineteenth Century* for December, the writer, evidently a medical man, states that a person once hypnotised is at the mercy of the operator, who can repeat the operation at will, even without the consent of the patient. Further, that anyone can easily hypnotize a person who has once submitted to hypnotism ; and again, that a person once hypnotised is unable to look people in the face without feeling an irresistible desire to sleep. I have made inquiries among my patients of both sexes, some of whom have been hypnotised many times, and have fallen into the profounder degrees of sleep. They can all certainly look me in the face for any length of time without feeling in the least degree sleepy ; and they all tell me that until they entirely give up their minds to the operation no soporific effect is produced. Most misleading conclusions have been drawn from exceptional cases, such as that of the 'Soho sleeper.' These belong in no sense to hypnotism as a therapeutic system, but are examples of hysteria. Constantly hypnotising a weak-minded person for experimental purposes will probably bring about a morbid state of brain, and such abuse of a therapeutic agent can only be deprecated and discouraged.

CHAPTER IV.

Psycho-Therapeutics not an exclusive System of Treatment.—Some Diseases found to benefit from it.—Organic Processes affected by Hypnotic Suggestion.—Blisters and *Stigmata* so caused.—Treatment especially useful in Neurotic Diseases.—Hysteria, Hypochondriasis, Dipsomania, and the Opium Habit.—Moral Depravity.—Double Consciousness.—Permanence of Cures.— Hypnotism distinct from Magnetism.—Possible Abuse of Hypnotism not a Bar to its Use in Medical Treatment.—Restrictions and Precautions necessary.

We are now in a position to speak of suggestion as a mode of treatment and cure, and we will first consider to what class of diseases it has hitherto proved applicable. And here I may say that, although Dr. Liébault rarely gives medicines, but obtains most of his remarkable results by the suggestive treatment pure and simple, his followers by no means dispense with those remedies which the researches of generations of able men have put within their reach. In suitable cases they make use of dietetics, drugs, electricity and massage, and the combination of these means with suggestion often gives better results than any simple treatment.

The suggestive method is especially applicable to chronic complaints. Rheumatism and gout often yield to it, as do also many diseases of mal-nutrition, such as anæmia and 'general debility.' In derangement of the functions in women it acts very beneficially, both in checking excessive loss and in promoting a proper flow; also in relieving or curing periodic sufferings of all kinds. In chronic constipation and diarrhœa it has excellent effects, and patients usually find that the intestinal functions become regular through its use. Indeed, therapeutic suggestion gives a healthy tone to the organic system generally, and tends to regulate all its functions. A consideration of the experiments of Bernheim, Delbœuf, and others will render this statement more comprehensible than it may appear on the surface.

Suggestion is extremely useful in cramp from the over-use of certain muscles, such as is commonly found among writers and telegraph clerks. It is very successful also in cases of old-standing paralysis, and especially so in the infantile variety. Many practitioners speak highly of its curative power in skin disease, and in affections of the eyes, and it is found beneficial in some forms of deafness. In fact, wherever we find chronic disease resisting the usual methods of treatment, suggestion may be thought of as a useful ally.

Its power over the organic processes has been clearly shown by many experiments, made either on students of the system or on patients, with their own previous consent. A patient in the hypnotic sleep is told that he has burnt his hand or some other part of his body; he not only feels heat and pain in the place indicated, but it frequently happens that the spot becomes red and inflamed, and exhibits all the objective signs of congestion, and even of inflammation, vesication, etc. The suggestion of the operator has, through the patient's imagination, been able to affect the vaso-motor functions of the sympathetic nervous system. This experiment and others of a like nature open up a wide field of pathological interest; for if suggestion can cause an increased flow of blood to a part, and local congestion and inflammation, can it not also dissipate and cure these conditions when they occur in disease? Clinical experience answers in the affirmative.

Professor Delbœuf, of Liege, desiring to ascertain the positive effect of hypnotic suggestion in the treatment of a burn, and being of course unable to find two persons of identical constitution and condition generally, used the ingenious device of producing, with caustic, two exactly similar burns on the same person—one on each arm—and of treating one wound by curative suggestion, combined with the usual remedies, and the other with the usual remedies only. Having induced hypnotic sleep, he suggested to the patient that the one arm should be cured painlessly and without any suppuration; and it did in fact heal, by simple separation of the slough and healthy granulation, ten days earlier than the other, which went through the suppurative process, accompanied by inflammation and pain (*op. cit.*, p. 9). Were this case not reported by a well-known *savant*, I confess I should feel some hesitation in recording it here; as it is, its accuracy is beyond doubt.

Professor Beaunis (*op. cit.*) notes a case in which, by suggestion, he regulated the pulse of a patient. Before sleep there were 96 pulsations in a minute, which during the sleep increased to 98·4. He suggested a reduction, and it fell to 92·4. The pulse having again risen to 100·2 he suggested an acceleration, and it further rose to 115·5. The slackening and quickening of the pulse in each instance followed immediately upon the suggestion. The tracings were taken by Marcy's sphygmograph; and of these facsimile reproductions are given in Beaunis's work. He also succeeded in slightly raising the temperature of patients by suggesting an increase of warmth.

He describes at some length the production of all the effects of a blister by suggesting that one had been applied. 'M. Focachon, a chemist of Charmes, showed us (Drs. Bernheim, Beaunis, and Liébault) this phenomenon on a patient whom he brought to Nancy. During her sleep, at about 11 a.m., eight postage stamps were applied to her left shoulder, while it was suggested to her that they were a blister. She was allowed to sleep all day, being, however, aroused for meals, and was kept under observation. When she retired for the night she was told to sleep until 7 the next morning. At 8.15 a.m. the dressing which had been put on was removed, and the stamps were found *in situ*. The surrounding skin, for four or five centimètres, was thickened, modified, and of a yellowish-white colour. The cuticle, however, was not raised, and did not form a blister; but it was thickened and wrinkled, and presented the appearance usual before complete vesication. This part of the skin was surrounded by a zone of intense redness and swelling. M. Focachon and the patient returned to Charmes, and by 4 p.m. four or five vesicles were developed. Fifteen days later the blister was still suppurating freely. M. Focachon made a similar experiment on another patient, and in forty-eight hours produced a blister, which followed the same course.'

Professors Bourru and Burot, of Rochefort, succeeded in causing hæmorrhage from the nose, by suggesting that it should take place, in a young soldier of epileptic and hysterical constitution; they even fixed the hour when it should come on. On this same subject Dr. Mabille, of the lunatic asylum at Lafond, produced instantaneously, by suggestion, hæmorrhage from different parts of the body, exactly similar in character to the *stigmata* of some mediæval saints.

It will thus be seen that suggestion is an exceedingly powerful agent—effective in the hands of the experimentalist, and efficacious also in those of the physician. When we consider that the knowledge of this treatment has only become general within the last four or five years, we must acknowledge that its progress, and the number of diseases which it affects, are both remarkable. But we must also acknowledge that it is no universal remedy, warranted to act like magic on all diseases. In some cases it is powerless, or comparatively so. It cannot restore a joint altered by chronic rheumatism or gout, nor put right an internal displacement, nor can it remove cancer or other malignant disease; neither will it cure paralysis agitans, glaucoma, advanced Bright's disease, or diabetes. Neither can it materially benefit cases of phthisis or organic heart disease, though it may do much to relieve the sufferings incidental to all painful affections. It has been but little employed in acute illness. I believe that most of the Continental practitioners of the system use it chiefly at consultations in their own rooms, where, of course, sufferers from acute diseases are not likely to present themselves. It has occasionally been used in childbirth, with beneficial results; but in surgery it is not often employed. No doubt a few susceptible persons might be painlessly operated upon while under its influence; but, as a rule, the natural agitation of a patient before an operation would so distract his attention as to render hypnotism impossible; whereas chloroform and other anæsthetics are easily administered, and are commonly certain in their effect. Professor Bernheim, however, uses suggestion in conjunction with chloroform, and finds that his patients take the anæsthetic better, and require a much smaller quantity, than when it is administered silently in the usual way. This is the experience of many chloroformists.

Suggestion may be usefully employed instead of narcotics in temporarily relieving acute pain, by inducing sleep which will not be followed by the deleterious consequences of such drugs. It is also used in cases where the sleep itself is remedial, as in threatening congestion of the brain, delirium tremens, and in insomnia, when it exists as an independent condition and not as a symptom of disease.

But it is in the so-called 'neuroses' that suggestion obtains its most brilliant successes—in functional epilepsy, St. Vitus's dance, asthma, palpitation, nervous headache, spinal irritation, neurasthenia, ovarian pain, and the many forms of dyspepsia. Nervous disease is, unfortunately, ever on the increase; and the study of its symptoms, its cure and prevention, must increase to keep pace with it. As civilization advances, humanity develops 'nerves,' which, in this sense, may be said to have no existence in the savage and barbarous states. The vices and virtues of civilization tend alike to increase our sensitiveness. Drink, narcotics, the abuse of tobacco, social excitements, intellectual culture, the ever-spreading desire to be or do something remarkable—these and many other stimulating influences are perpetually at work to promote nerve-disease among us. In large cities especially, where men live under artificial conditions and at high pressure, we find in all classes of the community affections presenting subjective symptoms quite out of proportion to the objective signs. It would be interesting to ascertain what proportion neurotic affections bear to organic diseases in a city doctor's day's work. Probably one half at least. Many of us when fresh from the hospital are vexed and surprised to find how much of our practice is made up of such cases. They are really among the most painful and difficult complaints a physician is called upon to treat, for they generally indicate a weak and depressed state of vitality, in which the slightest suffering is felt with intensified force. Take the medical nomenclature ending in *algia*: cardialgia, cephalalgia, gastralgia, myalgia, neuralgia—what visions of suffering do these words call up!

Though these affections often depend upon organic disease, they more frequently have their source in nerve irritability and functional weakness. How they perplex the able practitioner, who feels quite at home with a case of scarlet-fever or inflammation of the lungs! Nervous disease generally—hysteria and hypochondria in their many forms—are spoken of contemptuously by some pathologists, who are impatient of subjective symptoms which have no apparent objective reason for existence. Therefore we must not be too severe on the friends of hysterical and nervous patients, who, perhaps after long endurance of their complaints, grow intolerant, and, it may be, incredulous of their sufferings. It is natural to ascribe to imagination an ailment for which neither friend nor physician can find any comprehensible cause; yet these so-called fanciful ailments may be as real as typhus, and entail a thousand times more suffering on the patient. Bodily weakness, unaccountable pains, depression of spirits, a weight of misery accompanied by the conviction that no power on earth can lift it, a sense of being neglected by friends, or of being to them a weariness and trouble—all these sufferings of mind and body are real enough and hard to bear, whatever their original cause may have been.

There is no doubt that they are sometimes brought about by the patient's own fault. They may spring in the first instance from indulgence in bad habits, from idleness, from a tendency to foster and dwell upon morbid ideas; in short, they frequently are diseases *caused by the imagination*, which is quite a distinct thing from *imaginary diseases*. Indeed, there *is* no imaginary disease; he who persistently imagines a disease in himself *has* one, though possibly not the one he imagines. For the imagination which can furnish its owner with a bodily disease is itself not in a state of health. Who with healthy, well-balanced mental powers could or would bring upon himself a sickness by auto-suggestion? 'No one can be a hypochondriac at pleasure,' aptly says Lavègne.

'When one of those hypochondriacs,' write Binet and Féré, 'whom we are apt to call *malades imaginaires*, comes to seek the help of medicine, complaining of subjective pains and uneasiness, what do we often reply? "It is nothing; it is merely fancy; try not to think about it;" and he is sent away with some anodyne or simple remedy. This invalid, who has suggested to himself his disease, and who really suffers from it, becomes convinced that it is not understood, and that nothing can be done for him. The more he trusts his physician, the deeper is this conviction, and he who came with merely a chronic complaint may go away with one which is practically incurable.'

The disease induced by morbid auto-suggestion may be controlled and cured by healthy suggestion from without, given when the brain is in a state peculiarly receptive of outer influence. The mind of a nervous, hysterical, hypochondriacal person is usually shut against all outward influence, except such as corresponds with and feeds its morbid state. The patient when awake rejects cheerful and hopeful suggestions almost as if they were insults, but in the hypnotic sleep, his morbid self-influence being temporarily in abeyance, his mind will admit and act upon suggestions of bodily and consequent mental cure.

The suggestive system has been extensively taken up by foreign lunacy and mental physicians. Among these are Drs. Semal, of the Asylum at Mons; Mabille, chief physician of the Asylum at Lafond; Burckhardt, of the Asylum at Préfargier (Switzerland); these specialists and others frequently report cases of amelioration and cure through the use of suggestion in the *Revue de l'Hypnotisme*.

The insane are not easily influenced by hypnotism: all who have anything to do with them know how difficult it is to get them to fix their attention on anything except their delusion, but once an influence is gained over them, suggestion may prove most useful.

That border-land of insanity occupied by dipsomania, the opium habit, and the excessive abuse of tobacco and other narcotics, offers to the suggestive treatment an extensive field of usefulness. Professor Forel, of Zurich, in his address at the Congress of Neurologists, held at Zurich in 1888, gave it as his opinion that suggestion is a very beneficial, and often a very powerful, agent in these cases, frequently enabling the drunkard to take that first step, which is always so difficult, towards reformation and cure. He cited also several cases in which he had succeeded by its means in curing patients of the opium habit in from eight to twelve days, and that without the acute mental suffering which is commonly felt when an enslaving habit is quickly broken off. Drs. Van Renterghem and Van Eeden (of Amsterdam) likewise tell me that they have had great success in overcoming these moral diseases. At Nancy I had the opportunity of seeing many such cases in process of cure. One man came to Dr. Liébault completely shattered by indulgence in tobacco, which he both smoked and chewed. He was a railway porter, a big, strongly-built fellow, but he was weak and shaky through his excesses. His digestion was faulty, his tongue thickly furred, and he had no appetite. His pulse was slow and intermittent; he felt giddiness on movement, and his sight frequently vanished through incipient amaurosis. Persons whose nervous systems are broken down in this way are very easily hypnotised, and Dr. Liébault soon had this man in a state of profound sleep. He then told him that he was to give up smoking, that a pipe was to be to him an object of loathing, and a quid of tobacco even more offensive. Also, that if he did indulge in one or the other, pain and sickness would be the result, and that he must not even feel a desire for the indulgence. The patient came daily for several mornings, and daily showed an increasing improvement, till in a week he was completely cured of the symptoms of nicotine poisoning. He would, of course, have been cured by voluntary abstention from tobacco, but I doubt if the beneficial effect would have been so rapid—and no one seeing the man would have credited him with the moral courage and determination necessary for breaking off a long-cherished habit. It is told of the younger Dumas that he was formerly an inveterate smoker, and on one occasion, feeling out of health, went to consult his doctor with the usual cigar in his mouth. The physician, one in whom Dumas had entire confidence, having heard his symptoms, told him plainly that smoking was destruction for him, whereupon the great writer immediately flung away his cigar, declaring that he would never smoke another—and he has kept his word. But how many are gifted with such resolution?

In the *Revue de l'Hypnotisme*, 1886-1887, some papers appear by Dr. Voisin, of the Salpêtrière, showing the efficacy of suggestion in the treatment of moral obliquity; and at the Congress of the French Association for the Advancement of Science, held at Nancy in 1886, papers dealing with this subject were read by several physicians of eminence. Dr. Voisin gives instances of female prisoners, formerly considered incorrigible, who, after a course of suggestive treatment (combined with the religious and moral instruction which, alone, had unfortunately proved ineffectual), became modest, cleanly, and industrious. Some of these reformed women have been placed in situations of trust, which they hold satisfactorily.

In these cases a state of double consciousness,* such as one sometimes sees in natural somnambulism, was probably induced. A subject of this kind may live two alternate lives, one good, the other evil; and in one of these lives she will be unconscious of her actions in the other (Forbes Winslow, *op. cit.*, p. 420). In some instances both of these utterly different lines of conduct will appear so rational that it is difficult to decide which is natural to the subject.†

In course of time the new personality, induced by suggestion and encouraged by religious ministration and teaching, will displace the old, and a complete moral revolution will be the result. At the Nancy Congress, Dr. Liébault and others gave instances of dull, idle, and troublesome children being by suggestion (combined with judicious home-influence) made models of industry and good behaviour. A boy who at school had habitually been at the bottom of his form, was by this treatment so incited to work that he soon occupied a place at the other end. Another child, seven years of age, so obtuse as to be almost an idiot, was so benefited by suggestion, that in three months he could read, write, and do the first four rules of arithmetic.‡

Many people may object to the use of this treatment in moral cases, on the ground that it is a tampering with the free-will of those influenced. To this I would reply that

* Writers on somnambulism give many instances of this double consciousness.

† The story of 'Dr. Jekyll and Mr. Hyde' might be founded on one of these cases.

‡ See also page 61. In cases of *complete* idiocy, suggestion may be considered powerless, the difficulty of exciting the attention being practically insuperable.

all education and all exercise of moral influence are an interference with this free-will. Most children prefer play to work; some will tell a lie to escape punishment; all are addicted to a variety of faults and bad habits; and educational and reformative means of various kinds must be used to train them to industry, truthfulness, and general excellence of conduct. Where these ordinary means are efficacious, no others need be, or ought to be, employed, and it is only when they have failed after repeated trial that suggestion should be resorted to. As in bodily illness, the system should be applied only in obstinate cases and when other methods have proved ineffectual; so in the far more serious cases of moral infirmity should it be used as almost a last resource, and with the greatest caution.

One is frequently asked whether the cures worked by suggestion are of a permanent character. To this I reply, they are as permanent as cures effected by any other means. Relapses occur in many diseases, no matter what treatment has been employed; sometimes through some carelessness on the part of the patient or of those who have charge of him. A person who is cured of rheumatism to-day, may to-morrow get fresh cold and develop a new attack, or other symptoms. But with proper attention, and the customary precautions as regards diet, rest, temperature, etc., the success of this treatment is not transitory. The improvement effected by its means is often so marked and so rapid that patients are tempted to discontinue its use, and return to their ordinary habits before tne cure is perfected and the habit of disease broken, forgetting that when a diseased condition has existed for some time it probably has taken firm hold on the system, and is not to be dispelled in a day. Sudden cures are apt to be fallacious, as are such cures by other modes of treatment; and though brilliant results are sometimes attained they can never be counted upon, and there should be no disappointment when improvement is a little delayed.

On the very threshold a difficulty may occur; the

patient will perhaps appear insusceptible. This need not cause discouragement, for in many cases the hypnotic influence is not felt until after three or more séances. But very few persons remain insusceptible* to it; and when once it is established, the hypnotic state is afterwards more easily induced, and tends also to become more intense, though this does not necessarily follow.

It is very difficult to eradicate a deeply-rooted popular belief, and it is not very easy for a practitioner of the suggestive system to avoid being called a magnetiser, since artificially induced sleep is the common preliminary of the treatment. But, as I have already stated, Dr. Liébault and his disciples absolutely reject the fanciful theories regarding animal magnetism which were held fifty years ago. They contend that no unusual gifts are needed to practise the system, and that the chief requisite is confidence. (The above note shows how want of confidence may be detected by the patient, and how the very suspicion of it will cause failure.) With wider experience comes increased confidence in one's self and in the system, followed naturally by increased success.

But 'majus remedium majus venenum' is a true saying, and it would be an exception to all rule if such a powerful remedy as suggestion were not liable to abuse. When dynamite was discovered, no one denied that the lawless and desperate would, if possible, turn it to bad account, yet it was not tabooed for this reason, but its

* See tables, page 31. An apparent trifle may cause one operator to fail where another will succeed at once. I know a very able foreign physician who completely failed to influence two English patients, because he smelt of garlic, and so called up disturbing emotions in their minds. I was once unsuccessful with a gentleman, who afterwards told me the reason of my failure. He imagined, as many do, that it is essential for the operator to possess great strength both of mind and body. When I touched his eyes to close them, he observed a slight tremor in my hand, and attributed this to a physical or mental weakness, which, he argued, must prevent my influencing him—a stranger, and a strong man of high intellectual capacity. The idea called up a resistance, which rendered him insusceptible. Subsequently, when I had explained to him that my personal attributes were, in this matter, of no consequence whatever, he easily fell into a profound hypnotic sleep.

manufacture and distribution have been surrounded by precautions and restrictions, and it is allowed to occupy its proper place in applied science in the hands of miners and engineers. Sir James Simpson was not prevented from making public his grand discovery of chloroform because nervous people were afraid it might be employed for evil purposes; nor is its use forbidden, though every year a certain percentage of crimes and outrages are committed by its aid. Poisoning by arsenic, corrosive sublimate, and digitalis sometimes occurs, and yet these drugs occupy a prominent place in the pharmacopœia. For it is found that although these powerful agents are sometimes used to inflict harm, the evil caused by their illegitimate employment is so outweighed by their usefulness that no one would think of suppressing them. So with hypnotism. Its power for good is undoubted; it fills a place that nothing else can fill so adequately, and used with proper precaution and under necessary restrictions it is perfectly safe.

Dr. Sémal, in the discussion on hypnotism in the Belgian Academy of Medicine (June 30th, 1888), having condemned the prostitution of the system by travelling *prestigiateurs* and charlatans, spoke strongly in favour of having it included in the medical curriculum of the universities, as being the only legitimate means of making it known. 'This course,' he said, 'would prevent its being used empirically and stupidly, and would keep it as a powerful therapeutic agent in the hands of the medical profession as long as the art of healing is practised.'

The exploitation of hypnotism as an exhibition at public entertainments has already been prohibited by law in Switzerland, Holland, and other countries, and when the true position of the system is understood among us probably the same restrictions will be enforced in England. Such experiments are always useless and often cruel, besides being an offence against the dignity of humanity. The contortions and exclamations of a patient under chloroform are often interesting, and might by some persons be thought amusing, but we should hardly choose to excite them for the gratification of idle curiosity or the entertainment of the multitude.

The practitioner who uses hypnotism should do so with the same precautions which he adopts in administering an anæsthetic. Chief among these are obtaining the formal consent of the patient, and, when expedient, of his friends, and never operating save in the presence of at least one witness. Thus he will guard himself and his patient from all possible imputation of wrong-doing or abuse of power. I need hardly add that a patient desiring hypnotic treatment will, if commonly prudent, use discrimination in choosing a physician, and will avoid placing himself under the influence of one not known to him, at least by reputation.

The dangers of hypnotism are, I believe, exaggerated. The stories told of persons obtaining undue influence over others by its means are mostly fables, which experience shows to be impossible. Professor Bernheim asserts, and is borne out by other observers, that no one can be hypnotised against his wish, and that in fact it is his own will which sends him to sleep. Nevertheless, there is no doubt that after a time the on-coming of sleep is less under the patient's control, and when, as we see sometimes at Nancy, a person is continually being hypnotised by the same operator, the hypnotic state can be reproduced with surprising readiness. I believe that in certain hysterical cases there arises a craving for this, as there might for any other sedative; but such a craving has little chance of being encouraged if the suggestive practice is confined to its proper sphere. A physician does not go on prescribing narcotic drugs because a patient has a craving for them, but, on the contrary, forbids their use when they cease to be beneficial.

The physician practising suggestion may protect his over-sensitive patients from the dangers of being hypnotised by a stranger. He has only to impress upon them, while they are in the hypnotic state, that no one can produce any such effect upon them without their free will and formal consent. The most practised operator would try his art in vain upon one so protected, as Drs. Liébault and Bernheim have repeatedly proved,* and as I myself have seen.

I may fitly bring this chapter to a close with a quotation from Professor Bernheim's oft-referred-to work: 'It is the duty of the physician to select what is useful in suggestion, and to apply it for the benefit of his patients. When, in the presence of sickness, I think that therapeutic suggestion has a chance of success, I should consider myself to blame as a physician if I did not propose it to my patient, and if I did not even make a point of getting his consent to its employment' (*op. cit.*, p. 580).

* These physicians were in the habit of hypnotising an hysterical patient, who used to fall into somnambulism as easily in the hands of one as in those of the other. On one occasion, while she was in this state, Dr. Bernheim told her that she was not to be influenced by Dr. Liébault. She awoke quite oblivious of this suggestion having been made, and soon afterwards went to Dr. Liébault, who was ignorant of what had taken place, and asked him to hypnotise her as usual. To the surprise of both patient and doctor, all his attempts to do so were futile, and it was only on communicating the fact to Dr. Bernheim that his colleague found its explanation.

CHAPTER V.

Some Cases successfully treated by Hypnotism and Suggestion: 1. Aggravated Hysteria; 2. Hysterical Aphonia; 3. Chorea; 4. Hysteria; 5. Pseudo-paralysis; 6. Writer's Cramp; 7. Rheumatism; 8. Articular Rheumatism; 9. Neuralgia of Fifth Nerve; 10. Sciatica; 11. Nocturnal Enuresis; 12. Amenorrhœa; 13. Menorrhagia; 14. Partial Hemiplegia; 15. Hypochondriasis; 16. Puerperal Mania; 17. Hysteria and the Chloral Habit; 18. Moral Depravity; 19. Megrim; 20. Neuralgia and Hemiplegia; 21. Headache and Dyspepsia; 22. Chronic Alcoholism; 23. Neurasthenia and Deficiency of Saliva.

In this chapter I propose to give an extract of cases successfully treated by hypnotic suggestion from the writings of Professor Bernheim and others. Most of the reports are much abridged from the originals.

Case 1.—*Aggravated Hysteria for a year completely cured by Suggestion in Three Séances.**

Madame X——, aged 26; mother of two children. A lady of good constitution and lively temperament. She had not suffered from any symptom of hysteria until 1885, when an attack was brought on by some domestic trouble. From that time any annoyance induced a nervous crisis; otherwise she continued in good health.

Dr. Bernheim was consulted in October, 1886. The attacks had then increased in frequency and severity. They occurred about once a week, and were ushered in by a feeling of general weight and heaviness, and by a sense of constriction at the throat. These premonitory symptoms were followed by a deep sleep, which lasted from ten minutes to an hour. After this came general muscular tremors, which increased to strong convulsive movements,

* Bernheim, *op. cit.*, page 399.

alternating with general rigidity, arching of the spine, etc. On this stage followed one of muttering and hallucinations, loud laughter and gesticulation. After the attack had lasted from one to two hours it passed off, leaving great exhaustion and *malaise*, with complete forgetfulness of what had occurred during the fit. On October 19th Dr. Bernheim was consulted; he examined her and found nothing organically wrong. He hypnotised her, and she at once fell into a profound sleep. He suggested while she was in this state that there should be a disappearance of the malady, and that it should not reappear. On October 21st and 23rd she returned, and was again subjected to the treatment. There was no further need for suggestion, as the patient was cured and remained free from hysteria.

CASE 2.—*Hysterical Aphonia for Two Months, rapidly Cured by Suggestion.**

Madame C. L——, aged 30, has been hysterical since girlhood. On January 15th, 1884, having been voiceless for two months, she consulted Dr. Bernheim, who first applied electricity to the throat externally, affirming the while that it would cure her. As that, however, had no effect, he hypnotised her, and at once induced a profound sleep. He suggested to her while she slept that her voice should return, but on awakening her he found no improvement. The second and third séances were equally unsuccessful. At the fourth she slept more heavily, and Dr. Bernheim was able to make her say she expected to be cured in eight days† (the following Tuesday). He continued to hypnotise her daily, and each day he caused her to repeat that she was to be cured on the Tuesday. When that day came she was quite unconscious of having made this prophecy, she was still voiceless, and was hypnotised as usual. Dr. Bernheim told her she must speak when

* Bernheim, *op. cit.*, p. 427.

† In many cases it is most important to get the patient to fix a time for her cure; the idea becomes deeply implanted, and, in hysterical cases, it is generally realized. Of course, the sleep must be very profound to make this possible.

he awoke her, and impressed her strongly with this idea. On arousing her she said in a feeble voice, 'I think I can speak now.' The voice became gradually stronger, and by the evening was restored to its normal quality and volume. Dr. Bernheim gives many other cures of hysterical aphonia, several of them after one séance.

CASE 3.—*Choreic Movements of the Hands and Inability to Write, Cured by Hypnotic Suggestion.*

Victorine A——, aged 12½, of lymphatic temperament and good constitution, affected with chorea of the right

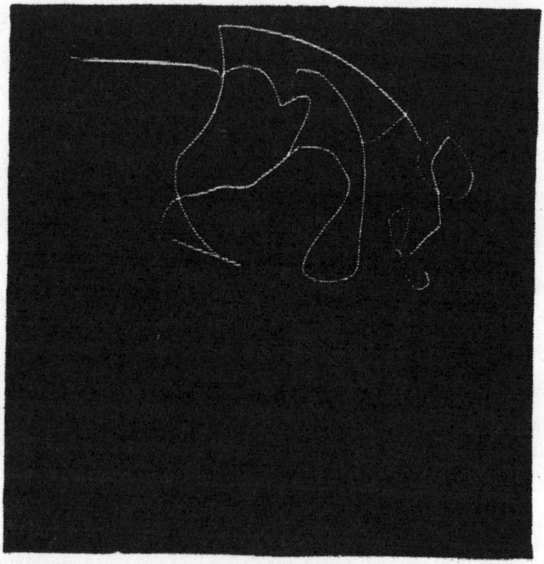

PLATE I.

side. It appears that when she was four and a half years old she suffered from general chorea, brought on by fright. It was a very severe attack, as she could neither walk nor talk, and had great difficulty in eating. It lasted three months. A second attack of the same kind came on when she was seven and a half. She was attacked a third and fourth time at intervals of two years. In the fifth attack she was brought to Dr. Liébault for treatment. It commenced on May 27th, and on that day she had seven very violent fits, on the 28th and 29th the same number, and then she was hypnotised for the first time. Afterwards, in the afternoon, she had two fits slighter than the preceding ones. On May 31st again hypnotised. On that day she had one fit, and then no more until June 9th, when she returned to be treated for a relapse brought on by fright. Professor Beaunis happened to be at the dispensary, and he got the patient to attempt to sign her name. In spite of much effort, the child—a very intelligent and docile little girl—completely failed to make any distinguishable letter on the paper. Dr. Liébault hypnotised her, and while asleep she was directed to write her name (Pl. 1). The result was fairly legible, and she wrote without hesitation or trembling. She was soon awakened, and again told to write. Without difficulty she at once wrote her name and address in very creditable style (Pl. 2). For the next few days

PLATE 2.

she continued under observation and treatment, and was then discharged perfectly cured.

Professor Beaunis says he makes no remarks on this case, as the handwriting appeals more than words can to an unprejudiced mind.*

CASE 4.—*Hysteria, Sleeplessness, Want of Appetite, Tremors, Depression of Spirits, Cured by Suggestion in Two Séances.*

Mdlle. X——, aged 27, an intelligent lady who had enjoyed good health and spirits, and was free from hysteria until August, 1885; at that time she had a disappointment which changed everything.

In February, 1886, she consulted Dr. Bernheim. She

* Beaunis, *op. cit.*, p. 236.

had then suffered for months from complete want of appetite, sleeplessness, giddiness, especially on lying down, terrible dreams when she did sleep, and slight muscular tremors in the limbs, so that it was not easy for her to keep her hand steady. She had been treated with bromides and antispasmodics without success. He hypnotised her, and she slept easily and profoundly. He suggested the disappearance of all her troubles, and after two séances all the morbid symptoms had disappeared, she slept well, and ate with appetite. Her spirits were as good as ever. Dr. Bernheim adds that she remained well.

CASE 5.—*Intermittent Pseudo-Paralysis of the Lower Limbs, with Convulsive Trembling of the Legs for nearly Four Years, Cured by One Hypnotic Suggestion.*

Madame S——, aged 26. After much domestic trouble and a bad miscarriage, this lady completely lost the use of her lower limbs for three months. The paralysis disappeared as suddenly as it came, but returned again in a few weeks. These intermissions and relapses followed each other every few weeks, up to the time Dr. Bernheim saw her, for nearly four years. She had undergone all kinds of treatment—including electricity and massage—at the hands of the most eminent neurologists of Paris, but nothing seemed to shorten the terms of paralysis or to avert them. On May 29th, 1887, Dr. Bernheim was sent for to Paris to see her. He found her perfectly free from the ordinary symptoms of hysteria, in good general health, without any organic disease, and unusually bright and intelligent. While lying down she was able to move the legs perfectly well, but when Dr. Bernheim made her attempt to stand she at once collapsed, and would have fallen to the floor had she not been supported. On moving the legs they were seized with tremors, over which she had no control.

He found the reflexes normal and all the functions perfect.

On being hypnotised she fell into a light sleep, during

which she was conscious of everything going on around her. On being aroused she denied having been at all influenced. Dr. Bernheim, while she was in the hypnotic state, moved the legs, and told her she would be able to stand and walk quite well when he told her to try.

After the operation he insisted on her making the attempt, and, to her surprise, she was able to both stand firmly and walk with confidence.

He hypnotised her again the next day, when she fell into the third stage of sleep, and the suggestions were repeated.

Madame S—— had been suffering from the present attack for six weeks when Dr. Bernheim was called in. He had opportunities of seeing the patient at intervals afterwards, and there was no relapse.*

CASE 6.—*Writer's Cramp for Three Years; Rapid Improvement; Temporary Relapse; Finally Cured by Suggestion.*

H. C——, aged 47, an accountant, consulted Dr. Bernheim November 18th, 1885. He was healthy and strong, and in no wise nervous or hysterical. Three years before he began to feel symptoms of the malady. After writing a few lines all the fingers became contracted, and he had to desist for a time. At first he was able to write again after a short rest, but gradually the cramp became worse, so that he was unable to sign his own name. By means of various devices he contrived to go on a little longer, but at the time he consulted Dr. Bernheim he had been compelled for three months to write with his left hand. He was hypnotised, and at once fell into the third degree of sleep. Dr. Bernheim suggested the disappearance of the cramp. On awaking he was able to write two lines and a half without cramp. The next day he wrote eight lines without cramp.

On November 21st the patient was able to write a business letter, and only complained of feeling heaviness in the wrist and a slight tendency to flexion of the fingers.

* Bernheim, *op. cit.*, p. 457.

On November 24th the improvement was still maintained, and Dr. Liébault took charge of the case during Professor Bernheim's absence for two months. In the middle of September a relapse took place, and the patient again became unable to write more than a few lines. He left off treatment, until January 29th, when he again consulted Dr. Bernheim. Improvement now rapidly set in and progressed until,on March 2nd, he finally discontinued treatment, being perfectly cured. He has gone back to his office, and writes all day long without fatigue or cramp.*

CASE 7.—*Rheumatic Pains in the Shoulder-joint for Three or Four Months, completely Cured in Two Séances.*

Emile L——, aged 61, glass-maker, consulted Dr. Liébault November 30th. He had never suffered from rheumatic fever, but nine years before had had sciatica for three years.

When seen, the pain was in both the shoulders, but especially the right one, at the place where the collar-bone articulates with the scapula. There was also a tender spot above the anterior superior spine of the ilium on the left side. It was most felt on stooping. Besides all this there were pains in both knees. The patient was hypnotised, and fell into a light sleep. On awaking the pains in the knees were gone, and those in the shoulder were much better. He had been unable for three weeks to dress himself, but now he was able to do so.

On November 3rd he was again hypnotised, and again slept lightly. He awoke perfectly cured, and remained so.†

CASE 8.—*Articular Rheumatism for Three Months, Cured by Suggestion in Two Days.*

Jeanne M——, aged 17, consulted Dr. Bernheim August 3rd, 1887. She was brought to the hospital in a

* Bernheim, *op. cit.*, p. 486.
† *Ibid.*, p. 539.

carriage, and into the consulting-room supported with difficulty by two persons, being quite unable to stand alone. She was lymphatic, pale and thin, and had had an attack of hysteria brought on by chagrin some months before.

Since May she had suffered from sub-acute rheumatism, which had gradually and steadily become worse.

Dr. Bernheim found that both wrists were extremely painful, but not swollen. The first joints of the fingers were greatly swollen and acutely painful on pressure. The left knee was slightly swollen and very tender. There was also pain below the right ankle and in the joints of the toes. The spine was tender on pressure.

There was also amenorrhœa, leucorrhœa, and sleeplessness. The patient was hypnotised and fell into a sound sleep.

On August 6th, after two séances, she felt very much better. She slept well, had a good appetite, and had hardly any pain. The swelling of the joints had almost entirely disappeared, and there was only tenderness on pressure. She was again hypnotised, and the suggestion made that she should feel no more pain.

On August 8th she returned completely well and cured of all the symptoms, was able to walk perfectly and without any pain, and was altogether a changed person.*

CASE 9.—*Neuralgia of the Fifth Nerve for a Year, with Tic-doloureux for a Month; Rapid Improvement and Cure in Ten Days.*

Charles X——, aged 60, entered the hospital July 27th, 1885. His trouble had commenced a year before with pain in the right side of the nose. The pain came on several times a day, and lasted from a few minutes to several hours. Since four weeks the pain had spread to the eye, the forehead, and all the right side of the face. It was

* Bernheim, *op. cit.*, p. 544.

very acute, and came on in paroxysms every hour or two, and lasted about half an hour. In the intervals there was no pain, but only a feeling of burning. There was lacrymation during the attacks, and they were also accompanied by convulsive movements of the face.

The patient was strong and well otherwise for his age. Dr. Bernheim found the points of exit of the branches of the fifth nerve sensitive to pressure, and all the right cheek tender to the touch. On July 28th, the first attempt to hypnotise him was unsuccessful; but on July 30th he was successfully operated on, and when he awoke he felt much better. In the afternoon he had paroxysms of pain, but less intense, and he slept better that night than he had done for weeks.

He was hypnotised about every second day until August 9th, by which date he was perfectly cured, and he remained well.

CASE 10.—*Sciatica for Seven Weeks, Cured by Suggestion in Six Days.*

Joseph L——, aged 44, shoemaker, was admitted into the hospital under Dr. Bernheim May 15th, 1885. He was a weakly person of lymphatic temperament and with emphysema. He had continual pain along the course of the sciatic nerve of the left side, and this was everywhere painful in pressure, aggravated by sitting, and especially by lying down in bed. The leg felt heavy and numb, and the pains, which were pricking in character, radiated from above downwards.

On May 20th he was hypnotised, and fell into the third degree of sleep. He felt better on awaking, and the curative suggestions were repeated daily until the 26th. Each day he became better, and in a week was perfectly cured. He had previously been treated with medicated baths at the hospital for three days without much effect.*

* Bernheim, *op. cit.*, p. 548.

CASE 11.—*Nocturnal Enuresis from Infancy, Cured by a Single Suggestion.**

Jacob S——, aged 17, of weak intellect, but strong and healthy, had always suffered from the above complaint. He had control over the functions during the day, but nearly every night he suffered from incontinence.

He consulted Dr. Bernheim December 28th, and was hypnotised with great readiness. Suggestions were made to him while in a state of profound hypnotic sleep that he should awake several times in the night, and leave the bed.

He returned to the hospital, but required no further treatment, for the malady was at once cured, and did not reappear.†

CASE 12.—*Amenorrhœa. Suggestion that the Function should Reappear on a Certain Day. Successful Result.*

Mdlle. C——, aged 25, teacher, consulted Dr. Bernheim November 17th, for the above-mentioned trouble. She had seen nothing since 7th October, and in consequence she felt distended, a sense of constriction round the waist, and other symptoms referred to the same cause. She was a regular patient of Dr. Liébault's, and she readily fell into a profound sleep. Dr. Bernheim suggested that the function should be re-established on November 30th, and made the patient repeat the suggestion after him.

On November 30th, she came to tell him that it had happened as he suggested. He hypnotised her again, and suggested December 28th for the next period. This also was realised.‡

CASE 13.—*Menorrhagia about every Twelve Days. Altered by Suggestion to Twenty-eight or Twenty-nine Days and Cured.*

Madame H——, aged 35, mother of three children, the youngest of which is nine years old. Hysterical, but of good constitution. Before she had had children the

* Bernheim, *op. cit.*, p. 495.

† All practitioners of suggestion agree that the system is absolutely specific in the treatment of this troublesome complaint uncomplicated by organic defects.

‡ Bernheim, *op. cit.*, p. 557.

period used to come on every three weeks, but for two years it had returned about every twelve or fourteen days, or even at shorter intervals. It was accompanied by pain and hysterical troubles, and was very copious. The patient readily fell into a profound sleep, and Dr. Bernheim suggested that the next should not come on until October 9th, should only last three days, and should not be accompanied by any pain.

September 27th. This was the fifth séance, and the sixteenth day since her last period. She felt premonitory symptoms of its return—such as headache, and pain in the back. These symptoms, however, passed off, and by means of suggestions repeated every second day the period was retarded until the night of October 6th and 7th, or twenty-six days. *This was the first time in her life that there had been more than twenty-one days' interval, and the first time for two years that it exceeded sixteen days.* It lasted three days, was unattended with pain, and was less copious than usual.

On October 18th Dr. Bernheim recommenced hypnotic treatment, and suggested that the next period should be on December 4th or 5th, and henceforth every four weeks.

It appeared at the end of twenty-four days. The treatment was continued until the following May, by which time the function was thoroughly regulated, and occurred every twenty-eighth or twenty-ninth day, without pain, or other abnormal symptoms. During the treatment a number of nervous and catarrhal symptoms disappeared.*

CASE 14.—*Partial Paralysis of the Left Side for Eight Days. Rapid Improvement under Suggestion, and almost Complete Cure in Three Weeks.*

Louis C——, aged 60, house-painter, was taken into the hospital November 7th, 1886. He had enjoyed good

* Bernheim, *op. cit.*, p. 560. The effect of imagination and emotion in modifying the renal, alvine, uterine, lacteal and other secretions is so well known, that the striking results produced by hypnotic suggestion in their functional disturbance is not to be wondered at. In 'Carpenter's Physiology' (*loc. cit.*) numerous examples are given.

health until six days before, when he had suddenly felt a sensation of weight in the left leg. He returned home, and two hours later felt the same sensation in the left arm, accompanied by a pricking, which still continued when he entered the hospital. In the evening he was no longer able to use his left leg.

Dr. Bernheim found the temperature and pulse normal, the arteries atheromatous and rigid. The features deviated markedly to the right. The patient sat up in bed with difficulty, and was unable to fully raise his left arm, which was also weak and easily tired. He was unable to stand. When lying down he was able to raise the left leg, but could not keep it up for more than four or five seconds. The reflexes were diminished, and he was unable to bend the instep. Sensibility normal. Constipation for four days, for which he was given an enema.

On November 9th the patient was hypnotised, and fell at once into a profound sleep. On awaking he was able to hold up the left leg for ten seconds, and to bend the toes better.

He was hypnotised the 11th and 16th, with only slight effect. On November 17th, after the suggestion, he was able to stand alone, and to walk with very little assistance.

On November 19th he was able, after being hypnotised, to walk the length of the ward without help. He could hold the leg up when lying down for an indefinite time, and had quite regained power over it. The reflexes were slightly increased.

He progressed steadily every day, and was able to walk downstairs on December 2nd. He still, however, felt a heaviness in the arm and leg, which prevented his using the brush or climbing ladders so well as formerly.*

Professor Bernheim fully describes one hundred and five cases of many kinds of disease treated by hypnotic suggestion. Among these are several examples of grave cerebral and spinal disease, in which the treatment

* Bernheim, *op. cit.*, p. 342.

seemed to prolong life, and of which it certainly relieved the suffering.

Examination after death often revealed a great amount of disorganization, so that it seemed extraordinary that any treatment could bring about much improvement. He explains the good effects which attend suggestion, even where there has been extensive hæmorrhage into the ventricles followed by atrophic changes, by insisting that in disease of the nervous centres, functional derangement often exists quite out of proportion to the actual lesion, *i.e.*, hæmorrhage may destroy a portion of the brain substance, and this may react on the neighbouring zones by setting up sympathetic irritation.

Neither suggestion nor anything else can, of course, do anything to restore the disorganized brain tissue; but it is all-powerful, he observes, in the treatment of the sympathetic and functional troubles which accompany such a condition (*op. cit.*, pp. 308-324).

CASE 15.—*Aggravated Hypochondriasis*

M. F——, aged 43, has suffered for a year from this malady. She is conscious of all her internal organs, and their functions cause her painful and distressing sensations, which makes her think that they are all more or less diseased. She has lost all hope, and is persuaded that she will never recover. She is debilitated and suffers from indigestion, does nothing but lament and analyze her sensations, lives in a perpetual state of agitation, and does not sleep.

She was put under suggestive treatment, and fell into a light sleep. By its means sleep was restored, digestion re-established, and, above all, her attention was gradually diverted from her sufferings, real and imaginary, and in a few weeks she was cured.*

* Dr. Burckhardt, superintendent of the asylum at Préfargier, *Revue de l'Hypnotisme*, August, 1888.

CASE 16.—*Acute Puerperal Mania.**

Madame X—— has had several confinements in quick succession. The consequent exhaustion, and an attack of phlebitis with fever, are the chief causes of the malady. After the first fifteen days, during which her life was in danger, the excitement and tendency to violent and purposeless acts were no longer continuous, but alternated with comparatively lucid intervals. Dr. Godet found that he could sometimes cut short attacks by suggestion. He suggested that she should remain tranquil, and should not open her mouth. In this way he calmed her in a remarkable manner, and the attacks soon ceased, and she was cured.

CASE 17.—*Hysteria, Tendency to Tetaniform Spasms, Insomnia, Morphia and Chloral Habit.*†

Madame K—— was admitted for treatment, suffering from the above conditions.

Hypnotic treatment combined with suggestion was employed to combat them. The narcotics were gradually discontinued, the spasms ceased, and natural sleep was regained by degrees, so that she was dismissed cured.

Braidism was tried without suggestion at first, but it only aggravated the symptoms.

CASE 18.—*Moral Depravity in a Boy, Cured by Suggestion.*‡

On June 9th, 1888, M. F——, a youth aged 16, was brought to Dr. Voisin at the Salpêtrière. From the age of six or seven he had been incorrigible. Not only did he tell lies, steal, play truant, and behave ill generally, but he also tried to corrupt all the children with whom he came in contact. He became worse and worse as he got older, and was turned out of several institutions into which his

* Dr. Burckhardt, superintendent of the asylum at Préfargier, *Revue de l'Hypnotisme*, August, 1888.
† Burckhardt, *loc. cit.*
‡ Voisin, *Revue de l'Hypnotisme*, November, 1888.

mother had procured his admission. (Dr. Voisin describes some of his vices, which are unfit for repetition, and which prove the youth to have been utterly depraved and bad.) On examination he was found to have an internal squint of the left eye, nystagmus, and haziness of the cornea. The tongue deviated to the left. Otherwise he was well-made and healthy. He read with difficulty, and was very ignorant, though his memory and power of observation were sufficiently good.

Dr. Voisin endeavoured to hypnotise him, but was not successful until the third séance. Once asleep, suggestions of moral reform were made.

He began to improve at once, and by July 6th the youth was absolutely transformed. The wish to do evil first disappeared, and was then replaced by a desire to do right. His insubordination and disobedience had given place to a wish to please his mother. He expressed to Dr. Voisin the happiness he felt at being thus changed. He saw the doctor again on October 6th, six weeks after the discontinuance of the treatment, and the cure was maintained.

Dr. Bernheim and Dr. Liébault give several instances of cures of moral diseases. The former, after describing a somewhat similar case to the above, asks if he can be accused of tampering with the child's free-will because he has repressed his bad qualities? (*op. cit.*, p. 357).

CASE 19.—*Migraine for Four Years, Cured by Suggestion.*

Madame A——, aged 28, a widow with four children, consulted Dr. Liégeios in September, 1887. She suffered from daily attacks of sick headache. She had two attacks daily, the first between 5 and 6 in the morning, and the second in the afternoon, between 3.30 and 4.30. Her health was deteriorating in consequence, and life had no attraction for her. She was easily hypnotised, and Dr. Liégeois suggested that there should be no pain that afternoon. She returned in the evening to tell him that she had passed the afternoon without an attack, and to be again hypnotised. Dr. Liégeois now suggested that there should be no pain the next morning nor henceforth.

At the time of reporting this case it was a year since he made that suggestion, and the lady has continued all the time free from migraine.*

CASES CONTRIBUTED BY DR. VAN EEDEN, OF AMSTERDAM.

CASE 20.—*Neuralgia of the Neck and Left Shoulder. Paralysis of the Left Arm and Leg, of Syphilitic Origin.*

A. H——, aged 34, is a strongly-built man, with an originally good constitution. He became infected eight years ago. Thirteen months ago he was suddenly attacked with total loss of power in the left arm and leg.

On October 9th he consulted Dr. Van Eeden, and was then suffering from severe pain in the neck and left shoulder, which had lasted two months. The pain prevented his sleeping more than an hour or two at night. He had partially recovered from the paralysis, but for five months no progress had been made. He was unable to fully raise the left arm, to open the hand, or extend the fingers. Antisyphilitic treatment had produced no effect for some months.

The patient was hypnotised in the usual way, and the second degree of somnolence (slight catalepsy) was produced. While in the hypnotic state suggestions were made to lessen the pain, and the rigidity of the semi-paralyzed limbs was relaxed by suggestions and active and passive movements. On awaking, the pain was found to be much relieved, and at night he slept four hours.

The treatment was continued daily for six weeks. By October 12th the pain had entirely disappeared, and he enjoyed eight hours' sleep every night henceforth.

Movements were constantly employed during the hypnotic state, and power gradually returned to the limbs, so that by November 8th the patient could extend all the fingers of the left hand, and keep the arm in a horizontal position for a considerable time. When treatment was

* *Revue de l'Hypnotisme*, September, 1888.

discontinued after six weeks he could make all the movements of the arm and hand freely. His walking power had also greatly increased.

CASE 21.—*Cephalalgia, Gastrodynia, Dyspepsia.*

The patient, a little girl of eight, is a delicate child, and has suffered from continuous headache, want of appetite, and pain in the stomach. She rises nearly every day with a bad headache, and twice or thrice a week she is obliged to stay in bed on account of the pain. The stomach pains occur irregularly, last only a short time, and are very severe. She never has had a good appetite. Once only has she been free from pain—about three years ago, for a fortnight.

On September 16th the child was hypnotised by Dr. Van Eeden for the first time. The sleep produced was profound, as is usual with children. In the first sitting the pain was quite removed by suggestion, and did not return for two weeks, though there was only one consultation. Since September 16th she has only twice had headache, and this was each time at once removed by suggestion. The child remains under treatment, as such cases necessarily require a long course. There has been no pain in the stomach since her first visit, the appetite is better, and the child's general health more satisfactory than it has been for years.

CASE 22.—*Chronic Alcoholism.*

M. G——, a well-to-do man of 49, had for sixteen or seventeen years constantly drunk alcohol to excess. He has never during all that time given it up. On his best days he has only taken four to eight glasses of cognac, but mostly he has drunk twenty or more. He has had several attacks of *delirium tremens*, and his mental faculties are much deteriorated. He is unable to apply himself to any business requiring thought or attention, and is unable to write his name. His face is covered with pustules of acne.

On September 27th he was hypnotised, and fell into a light sleep. Dr. Van Eeden suggested disgust for stimulants and increased strength of will. During the sleep the patient was persuaded to promise solemnly to leave off alcohol. He was also treated with arseniate of strychnia, four to eight milligrammes daily.

The treatment was continued daily for a week, then once a week for two weeks. After that no further suggestion was needed. From the time of the first sitting the patient took not a drop of alcoholic liquor, and though offered wine he refused it. Some restlessness and *malaise* were felt the first week. On October 4th he was able to write his name and to resume his business. Now (after two months) he feels quite well and strong, and is confident of being able to keep his promise. The acne is cured, and he sleeps and eats well. He continues to visit Dr. Van Eeden from time to time as a precaution.

In communicating these cases Dr. Van Eeden says 'they are selected from many similar ones. My results are the best in the treatment of various nervous diseases, but the cases are too long to report. I may add that according to my own experience the effect of psychical treatment is best seen in the following diseases: Neurasthenia, nervous debility, enuresis nocturna, slight or incipient brain troubles, morphia habit, alcoholism, bad habits in children, hysterical paralysis, nervous dyspepsia, anæmia, stammering, chorea, sleeplessness, nervous asthma. Combined with systematic movements during the hypnotic sleep, the treatment is also effectual in paralysis caused by apoplexy or embolism, and in infantile paralysis (poliomyelites anterior acuta), if not of too long standing.'

Drs. Van Eeden and Van Renterghem have practised treatment by suggestion among the upper and middle classes of Amsterdam for two years, during which time they have applied the system in nearly two thousand cases. They were both previously for many years in ordinary practice, and their testimony to the value of hypnotism and suggestion is therefore of great value.

5

CASE 23.—*Neurasthenia with Deficiency of Saliva and Constipation for Thirty-five Years, Cured by Suggestion.**

Madame V——, aged 55, consulted Dr. Burot in August, 1888. She had for many years carried on the business of weaving hemp, and it had been her habit to moisten the thread with the saliva. When about twenty years of age this secretion showed signs of drying up, and at the same time obstinate constipation appeared. She lost her appetite and became anæmic, constantly drowsy, extremely weak and feeble, and altogether a confirmed invalid. At forty the change of life occurred, but it made no improvement in her health, which became worse and worse.

Dr. Burot found her suffering from pains all over the body, general *malaise* and anæmia. The tongue was red and dry, with prominent papillæ. There was great dryness of the mouth, very deficient digestion, and obstinate constipation. The stools were infrequent, and their passage caused intense pain. The dryness of the mouth often prevented sleep. Dr. Burot hypnotised her and suggested increased flow of the digestive secretions, and at the same time gently rubbed the salivary glands and the abdomen.

After a month's treatment the patient was cured. The mouth became moist, the saliva abundant, digestion easy, and the bowels regular and comfortable. At the same time the general health was re-established, and she grew stouter and quite strong.

* * * * *

I had intended to add here a short chapter giving my own experience of the treatment, but the bounds originally fixed for the little book have been already exceeded, so I shall confine myself to a few remarks.

The results I have obtained in my own practice completely confirm the estimate of the value of suggestion as

* Reported by Professor Burot of Rochefort, *Revue de l'Hypnotisme*, December, 1888.

a means of cure which I had formed from watching the practice of others.

In many cases of neuroses—slight as regards the pathological signs, but serious enough from the patient's point of view—such as toothache, headache, rheumatic pains, neuralgia, gastralgia, etc., the relief has been almost immediate and most marked. In chronic cases, many of which have been under my care for years, I find hypnotic suggestion a most useful auxiliary in relieving pain, sleeplessness, restlessness, palpitation, and most other subjective symptoms. In the worst case of ulceration of the stomach I have ever seen, the patient, an anæmic girl, was immensely helped by it; and though it required milk diet and bismuth to make a complete cure, the duration of the disease was shortened, and the suffering attending it was mitigated to a very great extent. A case of telegraphist's cramp, of at least a year's duration, was entirely cured in three séances. In four or five cases of dipsomania, in both sexes, I have found it achieve results which nothing else could; and it is in the treatment of these 'moral diseases' that, I am confident, the greatest value of the system will be seen.

My opinion of its probable value in acute disease has been very much strengthened by a case I recently attended. A young woman, a particularly good subject for suggestive treatment, was apparently seized with rheumatic fever. Her temperature mounted to 104; she had acid perspiration, intense pain in the head and in many of the joints. The ankles and wrists were greatly swollen and very tender. The pain was so severe that she had had no sleep for twenty-four hours when I saw her, and her condition of mixed restlessness and weariness was distressing to witness. On several occasions I had hypnotised her for various troubles, and I now immediately attempted to produce sleep by suggestion. The pain, however, was so great that it took fifteen minutes to induce a light sleep. I left with instructions not to awaken her, and she slept for about an hour. She awoke refreshed, and slept at intervals during the night. On visiting her the next day I found the temperature 101, and the pains very much alleviated. This time she was hypnotised with greater readiness, and she slept for more than two hours. I suggested that she should awake free from pain, but I confess I hardly expected to find my suggestion successful. To the patient's great surprise, she was really free from acute pain when she awoke, and she was able to sit up and move the limbs without feeling anything more than stiffness and lameness.

In two days she was completely cured, and the rheumatic pains which had been flying about the joints for weeks did not return.

In this case, as in many others, the attainment of sleep without drugs was in itself of immense advantage, and the suggestions certainly removed all the pains of neurotic and sympathetic origin.*

My appreciation of the efficacy of drugs has been intensified since studying hypnotic suggestion; for I have seen on several occasions a properly selected remedy remove a symptom which suggestion had left untouched. Dr. Van Eeden has shown how the beneficial effects of massage and Swedish gymnastics are increased in certain cases by being combined with Dr. Liébault's system.

That hypnotic suggestion is destined to play henceforth an important part in the treatment of disease and the alleviation of human suffering is evident, and enlarged observation will show what it can and what it cannot do. If such a 'gift of healing' were allowed, in consequence of the neglect of men of science, to fall into unworthy and incapable hands, it would be a national misfortune and disgrace; but the truth has only to be pointed out to render such a consummation impossible. Of this I am confident.

* I have recently treated a case of partial insomnia. The patient, a scientist of great intellectual power, had for years been unable to sleep after 3 a.m., no matter at what hour he retired to rest. A short course of suggestive treatment has cured this morbid habit, and he now sleeps uninterruptedly, until 6 or 7 o'clock. This patient was only slightly influenced by hypnotism—*i.e.* to the 'first degree.'

APPENDIX.

Note 1.—For Page 9.

I AM informed on the best authority that in the initiatory rites of several secret societies the candidate is submitted to a somewhat similar ordeal. He is told that he must submit to be bled. His eyes are blindfolded, his arm is pricked, and a stream of warm water is allowed to trickle down it.

The surroundings at the same time being mysterious and awe-inspiring, a very great effect is produced on nervous and sensitive subjects. Syncope and nervous exhaustion not uncommonly follow the ceremony, and the new member may be made ill for days.

The rite is, no doubt, an example of the survival of the form after the unpleasant reality has, in deference to civilization, been allowed to fall into disuse.

Note 2.—Braid, of Manchester.

James Braid used to throw his patients into a kind of sleep or trance by making them fix their eyes and attention on a bright object—generally his lancet-case—held a few inches above the eyes. He found this caused fatigue of sight and abstraction of mind, which, in nearly all cases, induced the condition he termed *hypnotism.*

He practised his system successfully for many years at Manchester, and wrote several books in which he fully explained it.

But it seems to have died with him, and it is only now that *suggestion* with hypnotism has come so prominently before the profession that his works begin to be largely read. The most important one, 'Neurypnology' (London, 1852), has been recently translated into French by M. Jules Simon — an almost unique honour, I imagine, for a foreign medical author nearly thirty years after his death.

Braid found hypnotism increased the heart's action to such an extent that he warned medical men against using it when heart disease was suspected. He found it impossible to get children to keep their eyes fixed on his lancet case for the necessary four or five minutes, and therefore regarded them as insusceptible. We have seen, on the other hand, that suggestion finds its best subjects in children between the ages of three and fourteen, and in heart disease it is one of the most successful means of calming and reducing irregular heart-action. Braid went near to discovering the truth which Liébault, a few years afterwards, thought out, and introduced to the world.

NOTE 3.—DURATION OF HYPNOTIC SLEEP.

In order to arrive at the solution of this, Professor Bernheim allowed many of his patients to 'have their sleep out.' He found its average duration was three or four hours, but, as with natural sleep, it varied with individuals and circumstances.

On several occasions it lasted fifteen, and once eighteen hours. In all cases the patients awoke fresh and comfortable.

NOTE 4.—THEORY OF PROFESSOR DELBŒUF.

Among the numerous theories which have been advanced during the last few years to account for the influence of hypnotic suggestion in organic functions, that of Professor Delbœuf, of Liège,* deserves notice on account of its ingenuity.

He supposes that in an earlier state of existence the

* 'De l'Origine des effets curatifs de l'Hypnotisme,' Paris, 1887. See also review in *Mind*, Jan. 8th, 1888.

organic functions may have been under the control of the will and consciousness, but that in process of evolution the increasing influence and attraction exerted by the environment caused this controlling power to become weaker, and fall into abeyance.

In the hypnotic state the faculties are no longer occupied with external things, but may be directed and concentrated on one or more of the internal organs or functions. Then the power which has never been completely lost is again exercised for a short time.

As showing that control may still be exerted at times over organic processes, he relates how during a long dental operation he was able to restrain the salivary secretion by directing his attention and will to the function. The cases of Colonel Townsend and the Indian fakir, cited in Chapter I., also illustrate this theory.

Dr. Delbœuf goes on to say that in a state of perfect health the organs and functions work harmoniously, and it is to our advantage to know and feel nothing about them; but when organic life ceases to be normal, and when some function is deranged, it would be useful to be able to bring the will and attention to bear on the affected part. Hypnotism, by setting free the attention from the 'life of relation,' with which in the normal state it is preoccupied, renders this possible, and enables the mind to resume its knowledge, and the will its control.

Note 5.—Some Phenomena of Hypnotic Somnambulism.

Many extraordinary and, at the present time, inexplicable phenomena can be produced in subjects who attain the last degree of hypnotic somnambulism.

Such persons are but rarely met with, and are, I believe, always of hysterical temperament, which is generally combined with a tendency to phthisis, scrofula, or other chronic disease.

These phenomena, as has been already said, are of

purely psychological interest, and should be kept entirely distinct from therapeutic suggestion.

Among Dr. Liébault's patients at Nancy is a young woman named Camille, a favourite subject for experiment, as she readily falls into the most profound state of hypnotic somnambulism.

Like many hysterical persons, she takes a pride in her infirmity, and therefore, without being over-sceptical, one may wish to verify the experiments tried on her. One of the most curious of these is the production of *negative hallucinations* by suggestion. Camille, and one or two other persons of the same nervous temperament, would be told that on waking they would not see So and So, though he might speak to her, touch her, and even prick or pinch her, and the suggestion was realized. Or they would be told that the door was no longer existing, in which case, though apparently quite awake, they would seek in vain to cross the threshold until the spell was removed.

On my return to London I was fortunate enough to meet a lady who takes a great interest in the subject, and is at the same time susceptible of being thrown into the most advanced stages of hypnotic somnambulism. Her husband is a man of science, and also much interested in hypnotism. They were both quite ignorant of the phenomena I wished to produce, and the conditions therefore were perfectly satisfactory.

Mrs. H—— is about thirty years of age, small, slight, and a blonde. She is highly nervous, and occasionally hysterical, but she enjoys good health, is intelligent, and active in her household duties. On the first occasion I tried to develop a negative hallucination; her husband was confined to the room with a bad cold, and was sitting by the fire in an armchair a few feet from her. I hypnotised her, and told her that in waking she would not see him, would not hear him if he spoke to her, and would not feel him if he touched her. All this was literally realized. She was apparently wide awake, and yet when I asked her where her husband was she said she didn't know, but thought he had gone upstairs and would be down very soon. He spoke to her, calling her by name, and asked her to get his medicine, to stir the fire, what there was for supper, and a number of other questions. She gave not a sign of having heard; in fact, she evidently did not hear him, though she conversed with me intercurrently quite rationally. Mr. H—— then approached her, touched her hand, sat down beside her, and talked; but evidently for her he had ceased to exist, as she betrayed not the faintest consciousness of his presence. I then asked Mr. H—— to speak impersonally, and he said, 'Mrs. H—— will now go to the table, take up the doctor's gloves, and try them on.' She did not appear to hear, but in a few moments she got up, went to the table, and tried on my gloves—a thing she would never have thought of doing of her own initiative. I asked her why she did this, and she replied, 'I don't know; I thought I should like to.' She was not aware that the impulse proceeded from another. When I blew on her eyes and said, 'Mrs. H——, there is your husband close beside you, and you can see him now,' she looked fixedly at his chair for a moment, and then said, 'Yes, I see him now, but where was he a minute ago?' adding, 'At first he looked small and indistinct, but now it is all right.' We know we may look at a thing and yet not see it when in a 'brown study,' or preoccupied with something. A familiar example of this is afforded by observing how absent-minded people pass their friends in the street without recognition, though their eyes may dwell on them for some time. Afterwards they will deny having seen them, and truly they have not. 'Eyes have they, but they see not.' A physical impression has been made on the retina, but it has not undergone that cortical co-ordination or registration in consciousness without which there can be no perception.

I had only learnt that morning, from reading an article by Professor Liégeois* the curious fact that in hypnotic

* 'Un Nouvel état Psychologique,' *Revue de l'Hypnotisme*, August, 1888.

somnambulism the subject will carry out a suggestion made by a person whom she is prevented by some inhibitory nerve-action from apparently either seeing or hearing. The same lady kindly allowed me to try other simple experiments on her. She was ignorant of the nature of them, and only stipulated that they should not make her appear ridiculous or cause much pain. When in the hypnotic sleep I gently touched and kept my forefinger on a small surface of the wrist, saying while I did so, 'Poor Mrs. H—— has a nasty burn on her wrist, probably from some boiling-water; the place is very red, and rather painful.' In a few minutes I awakened her, and she immediately began rubbing her wrist as if in pain there. On my asking her what was the matter, she replied, 'I think I must have spilt some boiling-water on my wrist; it feels as if I had burnt it.' On looking at the spot, there was a very perceptible patch of redness about the size of a sixpence, and every moment this became more defined and angry-looking. As the pain was increasing, it would have been a breach of our agreement to protract the experiment, so I hypnotised her once more, and told her that there was no burn, and that the redness and pain would be quite gone when she awoke. In point of fact, a very short time was sufficient to disperse the morbid appearance, and on re-awakening her there was no complaint of discomfort. The same lady after the first operation complained of chilliness and stiffness, but I had only to suggest in future séances that she was not to feel these unpleasant symptoms to ensure her not being troubled with them.

These experiments belong in no way to therapeutic suggestion, but are of interest as they show how exactly the phenomena produced at Nancy may be reproduced by experiment in England.

Dr. Luys, physician to La Charité Hospital, Paris, showed some extraordinary experiments on a somnambulic and hysterical subject before the profession in October, 1888; and in the same month Dr. Vizioli gave a similar demonstration before the members of the Medical Congress assembled in Rome.

The importance of hypnotism as a means of investigating psychological problems is recognised by many eminent psychologists on the Continent. Binet and Feré, in their work already referred to,* say: 'Hypnotism seems to us to fill a void. . . . Associated with the clinical observation of mental and nervous diseases, it will give to the new school of experimental psychology the method it needs, and will furnish an explanation of phenomena based on experiment.'

NOTE 6.—DR. LIÉBAULT'S CLASSIFICATION OF HYPNOTIC SLEEP.

First Degree.—The patient feels a heaviness of the eyelids and a general drowsiness.

Second Degree.—This is characterized by suggestive catalepsy. When the operator places the arm in a certain position and says it is to remain there, it is impossible for the patient to put it down. It remains rigid and fixed for a much longer time than would be possible in a natural state. In these two degrees consciousness remains almost complete, and often the patient denies having been in the hypnotic state because he has heard and remembers every word which has been spoken to him. A very large proportion of people never pass beyond this stage.

Third Degree.—In this the subject is also conscious of everything going on around him to a certain extent, and hears every word addressed to him, but he is oppressed by great sleepiness. An action communicated to a limb is automatically continued. If the arm is rotated to begin with, it goes on turning until the operator directs its stoppage.

Fourth Degree.—In the fourth degree of hypnotic sleep the patient ceases to be in relation with the outer world. He hears only what is said to him by the operator.

* 'Magnétisme Animal,' Paris, 1887.

The *Fifth* and *Sixth Degrees*, according to Liébault, constitute somnambulism. In the former, recollection of what occurred during sleep is indistinct and recalled with difficulty; in the latter, the patient is unable to recall *spontaneously* anything which has occurred while asleep. All the phenomena of post-hypnotic suggestion can be induced in this condition, and it presents features of extraordinary interest to the psychologist.

Though spontaneous memory is extinct, it can be evoked by hypnotising the subject and asking him what happened in the previous sleep. Even in this rare and helpless condition, therefore, one has a check on abuses which can always be brought into use, and which might play an important part in legal or criminal cases.

A very well-known and scientific physician, Dr. Grazzini, of Florence, has been kind enough to send me the enclosed letter, giving full particulars of the case alluded to on page 20. It is so interesting, from a psychical point of view, that I feel impelled to translate and publish it *in extenso*, though it must be understood that such phenomena lie outside psycho-therapeutics as a system of treatment. In England we rarely, if ever, see such cases; but I believe that they are not uncommon among the Latin races. The hysterical Frenchman, known as the 'Soho Sleeper,' occasionally arouses scientific curiosity by indulging in fits of prolonged trance or somnambulism. In November, 1888, he had one of these fits, which lasted for thirteen days, during which time he was susceptible to suggestions of various kinds. Dr. de Watteville, for instance, made him the subject of delusions, in order, as he tells me, to prove to the police the indiscretion of allowing all sorts of people to have access to him.

In England we frequently hear of 'fasting girls,' and I imagine these cases fall into the same category as 'sleeping men.' As will be seen from Dr. Grazzini's letter, suggestion was actually curative in this case of 'spontaneous hypnotism.'

'The following case of spontaneous hypnotism may

interest you. G. F., of Alessandria (Piedmont), aged 32, of feeble constitution and delicate appearance, with a pallid and beardless face, is by occupation a travelling conjurer. I can easily hypnotise him by making him look steadily at one of my fingers and telling him to sleep. Occasionally he spontaneously falls into the same condition if a ray of light strikes his eyes when in the streets or when entering a brilliantly-lighted room.*

'I think it may be called a case of advanced (*grande*) hypnotism, for the various phases are developed in regular and characteristic succession.

'In the lethargic stage all the limbs are in a state of relaxation, and there is marked nervo-muscular hyper-excitability; the slightest pressure on or even touch of a nerve or muscle causes a corresponding movement.

'On raising the eyelids, he immediately passes from the lethargic into the cataleptic stage. He can then be placed in the most difficult and impossible positions, as though he were made of wax, and in these he will remain as long as desired without strain or fatigue. If the right eyelid alone be raised, that side of the body only becomes cataleptic, and the other side remains in the lethargic state, and *vice versâ* if the left eye be opened. Slight pressure on the top of the head causes him to fall into somnambulism, and in this state he is susceptible to suggestions. For instance, I suggested to him that on awaking he would be unable to speak or to move a limb; and this suggestion was realized, and his speech and movements were paralyzed until I removed the prohibition. Again, at my suggestion, he went to places which he did not know, and called on people who were strangers to him, at the hour and on the day I had named. He came to the studio of an artist friend of mine at the exact time I had suggested to him eight days previously, and on being asked why he did this could give no reason, and was surprised and annoyed at having gone there, for he had an engagement for that time at a neighbouring village.

* The man was subject to these attacks of spontaneous hypnotism previous to his having ever been hypnotised. The condition is not very uncommon among hystero-epileptics.—C. L. T.

It was on that occasion I induced a state of somnambulism, and suggested his copying a head drawn by my friend (alluded to on p. 21). He reproduced the drawing with the quickness and facility of a real artist; whereas his attempts at drawing when awake are childish scrawls, as you will see by the photographs I send you.*

'I determined to repeat on this susceptible subject the experiments shown by Dr. Luys before the Academy of Medicine of Paris, exhibiting the influence exerted by drugs on a hypnotised person at a distance. Without in any way entering into the controversy excited in the Academy by these experiments, I can only say that on holding glass tubes, which I had filled with tartar emetic or ipecacuanha, near the subject's back, he being in a state of somnambulism and ignorant of my proceedings, he was *invariably* attacked by nausea, agitation, and violent fits of vomiting. These symptoms ceased as soon as the tubes were removed. But when the tubes were prepared by a third person and covered with paper, so that I was myself ignorant of the nature of their contents, he no longer showed the physiological effects of the drugs used, but only vague symptoms, such as muscular contractions, more or less violent, or various emotions. I should add that these experiments were repeated in the presence of my colleagues and friends at the hospital of the "Fate bene Fratelli" (in Florence), to which G. F. had been brought, and where he was a patient in my ward.†

* Dr. Grazzini has sent me photographs of some of this man's drawings when awake and when in a state of somnambulism. He has also given me copies of his letters, written in his own person, which are what one would expect from a peasant; and others when, while in a state of somnambulism, he had been told that he was (1) a general in the army, (2) a grandmother, (3) a small boy. These letters are quite in keeping with the supposed position.

† The result of the deliberation of the Academy on these experiments was, that they decided that the so-called effects of drugs at a distance depended upon the subject in some way guessing the nature of the drug contained in the tube, and acting accordingly. In these highly nervous subjects the senses are wonderfully acute in somnambulism, and the slightest hint by word or gesture excites the *suggested* effect.—C. L. T.

'While in the hospital a large carbuncle developed on his right thigh, and, as an operation was necessary, I determined to avail myself of hypnotism to procure anæsthesia. A deep incision was made and the cavity was scraped and cleansed, while he was in a state of lethargy, without the faintest sign of suffering, and on awaking he had not the least idea that he had been operated on.

'I had observed that a magnet applied along the spine and to the head arrested the lethargic and cataleptic states, and it occurred to me that it might be possible to cure G. F. of the morbid tendency to spontaneous catalepsy which prevented him following his business and exposed him to dangerous or criminal suggestions.

'Accordingly I suggested that he should wear a magnet of medium strength tied round his neck, and that he should buy one as soon as he left the hospital. He followed my directions exactly, and for four months was unable to remove the magnet from his neck. During that period he had no hypnotic seizure, although he was constantly exposed to brilliant light in cafés and other places where he followed his occupation of conjurer.

'But, as usually happens, the suggestion gradually lost its efficacy, and when last I saw him he told me that he had had one or two slight attacks. I believe that by occasional repetition of the suggestion this tendency might be lessened, or perhaps cured; but my treatment could not be persevered with, as he left Florence, and I have lost sight of him.*

'Before bringing this long letter to a close I must add that I have used hypnotism *as a curative agent* in a case of St. Vitus's dance. The patient, a young man, had been treated with all kinds of remedies in vain, for the disease was most obstinate. He is now entirely cured, by suggestions made by me during the hypnotic sleep. He was

* In treating such a case, Dr. Liébault would certainly insist upon the patient returning at lengthening intervals until the morbid habit was overcome and displaced.—C. L. T.

allowed to sleep for half an hour at a time for twelve consecutive days.

'If you think these experiences worth publishing, pray do so, and they may perhaps serve as material for researches in psychology and therapeutics.

(Signed) 'G. B. GRAZZINI.

'FLORENCE, *December 13th*, 1888.'

THE END.

London: Baillière, Tindall, and Cox, King William Street, Strand.